[H.A.S.C. No. 114–42]

THE COUNTERTERRORISM STRATEGY AGAINST THE ISLAMIC STATE OF IRAQ AND THE LEVANT: ARE WE ON THE RIGHT PATH?

HEARING

BEFORE THE

SUBCOMMITTEE ON EMERGING THREATS AND CAPABILITIES

OF THE

COMMITTEE ON ARMED SERVICES HOUSE OF REPRESENTATIVES

ONE HUNDRED FOURTEENTH CONGRESS

FIRST SESSION

HEARING HELD
JUNE 24, 2015

U.S. GOVERNMENT PUBLISHING OFFICE

95–317   WASHINGTON : 2016

For sale by the Superintendent of Documents, U.S. Government Publishing Office
Internet: bookstore.gpo.gov   Phone: toll free (866) 512–1800; DC area (202) 512–1800
Fax: (202) 512–2104   Mail: Stop IDCC, Washington, DC 20402–0001

CONTENTS

THE COUNTERTERRORISM STRATEGY AGAINST THE ISLAMIC STATE OF IRAQ AND THE LEVANT: ARE WE ON THE RIGHT PATH?

———————

House of Representatives,
Committee on Armed Services,
Subcommittee on Emerging Threats and Capabilities,
Washington, DC, Wednesday, June 24, 2015.

The subcommittee met, pursuant to call, at 2:33 p.m., in room 2118, Rayburn House Office Building, Hon. Joe Wilson (chairman of the subcommittee) presiding.

OPENING STATEMENT OF HON. JOE WILSON, A REPRESENTATIVE FROM SOUTH CAROLINA, CHAIRMAN, SUBCOMMITTEE ON EMERGING THREATS AND CAPABILITIES

Mr. WILSON. Ladies and gentleman, I call this hearing of the Emerging Threats and Capabilities Subcommittee of the House Armed Services Committee to order.

I'm pleased to welcome everyone here today for this very important hearing on the counterterrorism strategy against the Islamic State of Iraq and the Levant [ISIL] also known in the region as "Daesh." ISIL or Daesh continues to spread and create instability throughout the Middle East, northern Africa, and Asia. Their propaganda insidious campaign of influence extends globally, manipulating or recruiting young men and women who are willing to die for Daesh. The trajectory we are on is not promising.

The President himself has acknowledged that we do not have a complete strategy to combat the threat. Defense Secretary Carter has acknowledged that the military is reviewing how to increase the effectiveness of our campaign and that an additional 450 troops would deploy to Iraq to expand the advise and assist mission. When I last visited Iraq in February of this year along with Representative Seth Moulton of Massachusetts, Elise Stefanik of New York, and Brad Ashford of Nebraska, there was talk that the Iraqi Army would begin taking back Mosul by the summer which now is leaving nearly 1 million people subjugated.

Today, sadly, we see this is not the case. While often characterized as a terrorist organization, ISIL/Daesh fights and behaves like an army. They remain well-funded and resourced, and we saw recently in Ramadi that they do not necessarily need overwhelming numbers to win on the battlefield, only an ability to strike fear in the hearts of those they encounter. Today we will seek answers to very simple but serious issues of national importance.

First, are we on the right path to defeat ISIL/Daesh? Second, what problems exist with our current counterterrorism strategy? And lastly, what other actions could be taken to counter this evolv-

(1)

ing national security threat? We will not answer all of the questions today, but what will be certain is the fact that it will take years to render ISIL/Daesh ineffective. Because of that, we cannot ignore the pressure of the declining defense budgets and the looming shadow of defense sequestration. As we examine our strategy against ISIL/Daesh, we must remind ourselves that if the defense sequestration continues, we will truly be fighting this threat with one hand tied behind our back.

We are fortunate today to have before us a panel of expert witnesses. They are, Ms. Linda Robinson, a Senior International Policy Analyst with the RAND Corporation; Mr. Michael Eisenstadt, the Director of the Military and Security Studies Program at the Washington Institute for Near East Policy; Dr. Fred Kagan, the Director of the Critical Threats Project at the American Enterprise Institute; and Mr. Brian Fishman, a Counterterrorism Research Fellow with the International Studies Program at the New America Foundation.

I would like now to turn to my friend, the ranking member from Rhode Island, Mr. Jim Langevin, for any comments he would like to make.

[The prepared statement of Mr. Wilson can be found in the Appendix on page 29.]

STATEMENT OF HON. JAMES R. LANGEVIN, A REPRESENTATIVE FROM RHODE ISLAND, RANKING MEMBER, SUBCOMMITTEE ON EMERGING THREATS AND CAPABILITIES

Mr. LANGEVIN. Thank you, Mr. Chairman, and I want to thank our witnesses for providing us the benefit of your experience and your insight. I know what you are going to have to say is going to be invaluable to the committee. And I look forward to today's discussion, certainly.

As we all know, we find ourselves in a very difficult circumstance when it comes to the interests of the United States and our allies and partners in the Middle East in the fight against ISIL. Our interests and objectives and those of our partners are not necessarily aligned. The ambitious U.S. strategy does not appear to be able to achieve the end state, but we are dealing with a serious enemy. And recent ISIL gains in Iraq and Syria demonstrate the need for a comprehensive, cohesive whole-of-government U.S. strategy as well as the cooperation of regional partners which has been challenged, at best, to enlist more support from our regional partners.

Now, while I share the frustrations of many about the seeming lack of a visible strategy, I'm not unsympathetic regarding the immense complexity of interlinked and sometimes contradictory challenges that the administration faces. We face a morass of gray when it comes to our menu of options, a ground commitment to the region seems to be a win the battle, lose the war option, but we also simply cannot walk away.

Similarly, swatting bad guys without a larger strategy in place really threatens to be another recruiting tool for our adversaries. So I look forward to hearing from our witnesses about what they think an effective U.S. strategy to counter ISIL should look like, and the situation fueling it across Iraq and Syria should encompass to achieve both near-term and long-term success.

Now, specifically, I would like to know what concrete actions you would recommend? What countervailing forces prevent these actions from being taken, and can those forces be mitigated? Are existing policies counterproductive? Can we have a coherent Syria and Iraq policy while negotiations with Iran are ongoing? What should postwar Syria look like? Are we able to align our objectives with those of our allies? And how do we engage more regions, nations in the region to be more proactive and involved in this strategy?

Are we able to align our objectives again with those of our allies? And how do we regain the initiative to make ISIL reactive rather than proactive? And how do we fight their narrative? What assumptions and desires will we have to jettison in order to achieve a workable outcome? And are we sufficiently leveraging the power of the non-military means, including financial, at our disposal?

So we have heard a variety of answers to these questions from the administration already, in testimony and otherwise, but I hope we can expand on our thinking here today. I am under no illusions that if we only change a few things about the United States approach to the region, peace will somehow instantly break out tomorrow.

We must recognize that we are in a highly complex generational struggle against those who would pervert one of the world's great religions into a justification for the murder of thousands of innocents, including women and children, and the wanton destruction of an incredible piece of a shared human heritage in a region already gripped by a terrible humanitarian crisis born from years of strife and conflict.

With today's discussion, I hope we can explore what a more peaceful region would look like and require, and ensure that our actions today and tomorrow are aligned in working towards a sustainable solution.

So with that, Mr. Chairman, I want to thank you for holding this hearing, and the witnesses you have arranged to testify today, and with that, I yield back.

Mr. WILSON. Thank you very much, Mr. Langevin. And I agree with you that we are in a generational conflict. And I look forward to working with you in a bipartisan manner on these issues.

We are joined today at some time with Representative Martha McSally of Arizona, and Representative Mike Coffman of Colorado, who is here. They are members of the House Armed Services Committee, but not part of this subcommittee. So I ask unanimous consent that non-subcommittee members be allowed to participate in today's hearing after all subcommittee members have had the opportunity to ask questions. Is there any objection?

Without objection, non-subcommittee members will be recognized at the appropriate time with each member here under the 5-minute constraint.

Ms. Robinson, thank you again for being here today, and we look forward beginning with your testimony, and for the benefit of persons who are attending today, and I'm just grateful to see the number of people who are interested.

It's a 5-minute section for each one of you. Then each member of the subcommittee will have the opportunity for 5 minutes. And all of us are going to be a person beyond any characterization of inappropriate, and that is Pete Villano is going to keep the time, so as professional staff of the Armed Services Committee. So we are very fortunate to have such a capable person. Ms. Robinson.

STATEMENT OF LINDA ROBINSON, SENIOR INTERNATIONAL POLICY ANALYST, RAND CORPORATION

Ms. ROBINSON. Thank you, Chairman Wilson, Ranking Member Langevin, and members. Thank you for inviting me to speak on these important topics. I returned from Iraq 10 days—3 weeks ago from 10 days in Iraq and Jordan. This was my second research trip to the region this year. I will first address the military line of operations, then recommendations for improving the strategy that is currently in place, and finally, comment on the alternatives.

My bottom line: The best option is the partnered approach because indigenous ground forces are required to defeat this formidable hybrid enemy in a lasting way. However, the ways and means currently applied are inadequate on both the U.S. and the Iraqi side. Syria is a much harder case, but there the alliance of the People's Protection Units and Free Syria Army may have potential.

My prepared remarks include a detailed assessment of the five forces fighting ISIL in Iraq. I conclude that separately, they cannot defeat ISIL. But together, they might. Currently, however, they are stovepiped and inadequately coordinated and supported. The following suite of measures, if implemented quickly and in tandem, might achieve significant effect in the short term.

U.S. advisors should be pushed out to all area commands in ISIL-threatened territory. They should also be allowed to embed with capable and trusted brigades such as the Counter-Terrorism Service and to move forward as needed to their command posts. Sending 450 advisors to Anbar was a first step, but belated. It had been urged months ago. Advisors cannot be effective if pushed out on the eve of battle. It takes time to gain enemy and friendly situational awareness, plan and conduct operations, conduct tribal engagement, coordinate artillery and air support, and gain influence to restrain abuses.

My second recommendation is that U.S. Special Operations Forces [SOF] have their request granted immediately. They have requested Exelis satellite radios that are in U.S. Army stocks in Kuwait, and they want to give these to Iraqi units. These radios instantly and accurately mark the unit's location, and together with U.S. joint terminal air controllers [JTAC] at the brigade and area commands, this could have a transformative effect. The people I talked to in Iraq, however, did not argue for putting the joint terminal air controllers at the battalion and below level.

One reason is that this would entail a much larger footprint for quick reaction forces, medevac [medical evacuation], air support, and logistic support, and the certainty of U.S. troops being in contact with the enemy. Many SOF officers also have come to believe that this ultimately increases dependency.

My third recommendation is that the Baghdad combined operations center, the current nerve center of our effort in Baghdad, needs to focus more on coordination and planning at the national level rather than act primarily as a strike cell.

My fourth recommendation is that the needed vehicles and heavy weapons be expedited to Iraq. The depots are full of small arms and ammunition, and in particular, I would urge that the Iraqi Counter-Terrorism Service needs be met immediately. They have been carrying the load of the fighting as some of you may know, they have been heavily attrited with over 2,600 casualties although they are now in the process of rebuilding. They will reach their assigned level of 11,000 by next January.

Finally, the air campaign could be made more effective within the current ROE [rules of engagement] by certain measures including increased ISR [intelligence, surveillance, and reconnaissance], more deliberate targeting, and additional target engagement authorities. For Iraq's part, it must incorporate more Sunnis into both the popular mobilization forces and the army. Sunnis, thousands of Sunnis want to fight. I met with a number of Tikritis who fought spontaneously to liberate Tikrit, but they now have no support. Passage of the National Guard legislation would be extremely helpful if it gives provincial governors a role. This would also regularize command and control of local Shia and Sunni forces for the long-term.

Third, Iraq must commit to recruiting those forces or others into the Iraqi Army, put good leaders into key posts, and shift the current disposition which is heavily arrayed around Baghdad and in Shia areas. In return I believe the U.S. should support a long-term rebuilding of the ISF, the Iraqi Security Forces, because the alternative is Lebanonization, the entrenchment of militias.

Iraq may dissolve, or it may find its way to a decentralized state. But taking actions that hasten that dissolution, such as unilaterally creating a large army of tribal forces could fuel further conflict. We have been down that road. The partnered approach may not work. We may be forced to fall back to containment. Though I believe that may be no more effective. I would not give up on the current partnered approach without aggressively implementing it and staying that course for some time. Thank you very much.

Mr. WILSON. And thank you, Ms. Robinson, very much.

[The prepared statement of Ms. Robinson can be found in the Appendix on page 31.]

Mr. WILSON. Mr. Eisenstadt.

STATEMENT OF MICHAEL EISENSTADT, DIRECTOR, MILITARY AND SECURITY STUDIES PROGRAM, THE WASHINGTON INSTITUTE FOR NEAR EAST POLICY

Mr. EISENSTADT. Chairman Wilson, Ranking Member Langevin, distinguished members of the subcommittee, thank you for giving me this opportunity to appear before you today to discuss the counter-ISIL campaign.

Recent gains by ISIL in Iraq and Syria mark major setbacks in the 10-month-old campaign against the group and highlight fundamental flaws in the administration's strategy that need to be rectified if the coalition is to succeed. To ensure success in what will inevitably be a long struggle, the U.S. needs to first, address the means-ends mismatch in its strategy; second, bring its own policies and those of its allies into alignment with the strategy. And third, undermine the appeal of ISIL by ensuring the defeat of its military forces and the dismantling of its state.

Now, first with regard to the means-ends mismatch. The U.S. has devoted inadequate resources in pursuit of what is for now an unrealistic goal, destroying ISIL. The U.S. needs to ramp up its efforts while lowering its sights, at least in the near term, regarding an organization that has demonstrated impressive regenerative powers. Its resilience is rooted in ideological and organizational factors and the characteristics of the Middle Eastern operational environment. Ideologically, ISIL supporters are unbothered by the criticism of establishment Muslim clerics whom they regard as servants of an illegitimate state system. Thus, efforts to delegitimize ISIL on religious grounds are likely to succeed only on the margins. Organizationally, ISIL can draw on manpower reserves from around the world and it has recently started establishing overseas affiliates, ensuring the survival of the ISIL brand, even if its flagship operation in Iraq and Syria is defeated.

As for the operational environment, the proliferation of weak and failing states and the region's zero-sum politics ensure the survival of groups like ISIL. Thus, while coalition military operations may be attriting and in places rolling back ISIL forces, the coalition has not degraded the overall capabilities of an organization that remains on the offensive in a number of critical fronts. In terms of aligning policies and strategy, the United States and its partners have often pursued policies that have strengthened Salafi-jihadist groups such as ISIL, thereby undermining the U.S.-led campaign.

First of all, American inaction in the face of the Syrian civil war, the Maliki regime's sectarian politics in Iraq, the widespread perception in the region that the United States is tacitly aligned with Iran, and the fact that America's first military strikes in Iraq were to save Yazidis, Turkmen, and Kurds, anybody but Sunni Arabs—all of these were a recruiting boon for Salafi-jihadist groups such as ISIL.

Secondly, the United States insists that it is training and equipping the moderate Syrian opposition to fight ISIL while the opposition as well as America's partners to this effort want to fight the al-Assad regime. And this is a recipe for disaster.

Third, the success of America's counter-ISIL strategy is hostage to its regional partners whose politics created the conditions for the rise of violent jihadist groups such as ISIL and Jabhat al-Nusra.

Fourth, the United States will not succeed in its fight against ISIL in Iraq if it does not succeed in its fight against ISIL in Syria, where it enjoys a safe haven that it will use to threaten and undermine the state of Iraq.

But it is not too late to correct course. So what is to be done? The solution is not another major U.S. ground operation that, absent changes in the region's politics would likely have to be repeated several years hence, but neither can we afford to walk away from the problem. The answer is rebalancing the administration's light footprint approach.

Thus, the U.S. should close the means-ends gap by ramping up its advise-and-assist mission in Iraq and its train-and-equip effort in Syria, rethinking its approach to training Iraqis and Syrians, intensifying its air campaign and preventing additional reverses as recently occurred in Ramadi and Palmyra. New victories for ISIL, even if ephemeral, will be fatal to the efforts convincing the Arabs sitting on the fence in Iraq to join the coalition against ISIL.

The goal should be to overextend ISIL by pressuring it simultaneously in Iraq and Syria, thereby rendering it vulnerable to internal uprisings and external attack. However, closing the means-ends gap is not sufficient for success. The United States also needs to alter its policies and those of its partners that have undermined the military effort. The dependence of the U.S. strategy on its allies' willingness to alter their politics and policies is our strategy's Achilles heel.

And finally, with regard to undermining ISIL's appeal, because so much of ISIL's appeal derives from its aura of military invincibility, its defeat would show that ISIL is just another failed ideological movement that brought only ruin to its supporters. Its defeat would mean no caliphate, no Islamic utopia, no glory and adventure, and none of the other things that have drawn so many to embrace it. The defeat of ISIL is, thus, key to undermining its appeal, discrediting its ideology, and demolishing its brand. And this, ultimately, is the most important goal of the counter-ISIL military campaign. But the administration's current light footprint approach permits ISIL to continue to accrue victories that undercut this effort.

Now one final thought. The U.S. and its partners need to figure out how Al Qaeda and its affiliates as well as Iran fit into all of this. For if the coalition enfeebles or defeats ISIL, which is still a long way away, only to clear the way for the primacy of Jabhat al-Nusra in Syria and expansion of Iranian regional influence, the United States will have only succeeded in further fueling the region's ranging sectarian and geopolitical conflicts. The sooner Washington realizes this, the sooner it can work to avert an even greater disaster that it may be inadvertently abetting. Thank you.

Mr. WILSON. Thank you very much, Mr. Eisenstadt.

[The prepared statement of Mr. Eisenstadt can be found in the Appendix on page 50.]

Mr. WILSON. And Dr. Fred Kagan.

STATEMENT OF DR. FREDERICK W. KAGAN, CHRISTOPHER DEMUTH CHAIR AND DIRECTOR, CRITICAL THREATS PROJECT, AMERICAN ENTERPRISE INSTITUTE

Dr. KAGAN. Thank you, Mr. Chairman. Thank you very much for calling this hearing. And thank you to all of the members for attending and for giving this important issue your thought when there's so many other things going on.

I agree with the ranking member, this is very hard. And I also have a lot of sympathy with anyone, including the administration, struggling to come up with a strategy to deal with this problem. And I do think there is a lot of room for reasonable people to disagree.

I have offered in my testimony a fair amount of detail about what I think should be done in Iraq and what we might hope to achieve. I would like for the few minutes that I have here, to address what I think is a conceptual problem in the way that we have been discussing this matter, or one of several. And that is the continued refrain that there is no military solution to this problem. Of course there is no military solution to this problem. War is an extension of politics. There is never a purely military solution, or almost never, to a military conflict.

However, this is a war, and any solution has to have a military component. And I think that we are too often conflating these two issues and not paying enough heed to what is required of the military component of any strategy that might be successful while telling ourselves that there is not a military solution. And I'm not offering a military solution.

But I think that we are generally underestimating what is required of the military component of any strategy and although I would associate myself with almost everything that my previous two colleagues have said, I disagree with the notion that a larger footprint would create dependency or would be unwise. And I very much disagree with the notion that it is desirable to keep U.S. forces from engaging in combat with the enemy if our objective is to defeat this enemy and maintain and establish a solid alliance with Iraqis.

It is extraordinarily hard to establish your bona fides as an ally if your position is, hey, we are going to watch you guys go out and fight. Let us know how that goes. And at the end of the day, we really need to think hard about this. Are we in this or not? Is this our war, or isn't it? If it is, then we need to be prepared to have our people serve alongside of Iraqis, not as they did in 2007, 2008, 2009. I'm not advocating putting combat brigades in and taking the fight away from the Iraqis.

I entirely agree that partnership is the correct model. I think we probably need to partner down to lower levels. But that is something that I would be reasonably comfortable leaving up to commanders in the field, if they were given the discretion to make those calls. I think that having a black and white national level decision that says we are not going to do that, I think it's the wrong decision, and I think it handicaps our forces too much.

I also think that we have a problem when we say there is no military solution, what's the political solution? In that we break in our minds what is in fact a real close relationship between those two things on the ground. The political situation in Iraq isn't just whatever the political situation in Iraq is. It is affected by what we do. It is affected by the military situation. It is affected by the actions we take. It is affected by what we actually offer.

We don't like the fact that the Iraqis are too dependent on Iran. I don't like that. I understand why they are. We are not offering them enough to make it a reasonable bet to turn down what the Iranians are offering them and anger the Iranians to some extent and rely instead on us. Now, it may be that they wouldn't anyway, and it may be that we can't offer them enough, and so on, and so on.

But as Linda Robinson said very eloquently, we have continually failed to try to do a number of things that where there was a reasonable expectation that they might succeed, and as long as we continue to fail to try to do things that have worked before, in admittedly different circumstances, we are going to continue to chase this.

And so I think we need to understand that we need to see the military component of any solution as an element of the larger solution that interacts with the entire solution and understand that we have the potential to change the situation in ways that can also change the political discourse.

And lastly, I would like to just make a brief comment on the subject of minimalism and the belief that we really should send in only as many forces, precisely try to titrate exactly how many forces we need on the ground and not have a single soldier there more than is necessary, which is, I recognize, not what my colleagues are advocating.

It is a mistake to take that approach. Unexpected things happen. Ramadi comes under attack. Ramadi falls. You have setbacks in war. The truth of the matter is that if you do believe this is a war and if you do believe that we are in it, then you should also—you also have to believe that we need to make available the forces that are required and forces that might be required in dire circumstances should they arise. Thank you very much.

Mr. WILSON. Thank you very much, Dr. Kagan.

[The prepared statement of Dr. Kagan can be found in the Appendix on page 59.]

Mr. WILSON. Mr. Fishman.

STATEMENT OF BRIAN FISHMAN, COUNTERTERRORISM RE-SEARCH FELLOW, INTERNATIONAL STUDIES PROGRAM, NEW AMERICA FOUNDATION

Mr. FISHMAN. Thank you, Chairman Wilson, Ranking Member Langevin, members of the committee. Thank you for having me here.

The Islamic State is a hybrid organization that aims to establish an extremely harsh form of Islamic law across much of the world. And to advance that goal it has five essential lines of effort. It is establishing a proto-state at the moment in Iraq and Syria. It is waging military campaigns to advance that in those two places. It is encouraging followers to independently attack hostile governments in the West, in the U.S. and Western Europe. It is building a network of affiliates, working to establish similar government structures around the world, and critically, as Mike Eisenstadt said, it is inspiring jihadis around the world to enter this organization, or to at least endorse its vision of a caliphate. We have to fight against all of these lines of effort if we are going to succeed against this organization.

Critically, ISIS' [Islamic State of Iraq and Syria] fundamental goal and its basic operational vectors, with the exception of building an affiliate network and expanding its core operations to Syria, have been relatively consistent since October of 2006. In Washington we have continued to fail to recognize the persistence of this organization going back to the declaration of what was then called the Islamic State of Iraq.

We don't often recognize our long history fighting ISIS, but we have effectively been fighting this organization for a decade already. And it is because of our sustained fight to this date that I, unfortunately, believe that our fight in the future is going to take at least another decade. And we need to be thinking about whatever policy we pursue it needs to be sustainable. It needs to be something that doesn't just stop. The worst mistakes we can make are to make a commitment and then pull away.

From 2006 to 2008 we fought ISIS effectively, but we failed to destroy it. The "surge" of 150,000 American troops into Iraq is a top line number, including crucial special operators and a concerted effort to inspire the Awakening of Sunni tribes against the Islamic State of Iraq eliminated its ability to control territory and forced it to abandon large-scale insurgent and conventional military operations.

Nonetheless, the group was not defeated. It remained one of the deadliest terrorist organizations in the world. It was continually from that period forward viewed by jihadis globally as the kernel of a future caliphate. It maintained a strong presence near Mosul, Iraq, throughout the period and in Syrian border areas. It established the bureaucratic structure for future governance and it sustained the ability to play spoiler in Iraqi politics by assassinating Sunnis and using terrorist attacks to encourage the Shia-dominated Maliki government into embracing its sectarian demons.

There are some key lessons from that era that we should remember today as we think about our future strategy. One is that ISIS is vulnerable to military pressure. Despite its growth, the group's convention military power is limited and it can be disrupted with military power.

Second is, ISIS is extremely resilient. It can shift its geographic base of operations and mode of organization relatively quickly. Operational setbacks will impact ISIS' global appeal, but the group will remain a viable caliphate to its supporters so long as it controls territory and continues to fight. And that means really any territory. It was continually viewed as a future caliphate even in 2009 and 2010 and 2011 at its weakest moment.

And even a diminished ISIS can operate as a political spoiler in Iraq and Syria. So what should we do in the future? ISIS will not be defeated so long as the Syrian civil war continues and Sunnis in Iraq live in mortal fear of their own government. Military action can contain ISIS and limit its ability to control territory and people, but such gains will be inadequate and fleeting without political resolutions in Syria and Iraq. The ugly reality is that the United States does not have policy levers to defeat the Islamic State in the near term without massive, and in my opinion, politically untenable intervention in both Iraq and Syria.

This is going to be a long fight and our strategy has to be calibrated such that it is sustainable. So rather than scope an entire strategy, I'm going to just point to a couple of present issues. One, should the United States support Syrian rebels focused on deposing Assad, in addition to those focused on destroying ISIS? The answer is yes. And this is something that I have not believed continually, but I have come to this opinion. Although this approach carries significant risks such as increased Iranian troublemaking and weapons falling into jihadi hands, it will bolster relationships with our allies in the region including and especially Turkey, and increase pressure on the Assad regime to accept political compromise.

That said we should not under any circumstances legitimize Al Qaeda-linked jihadi groups like Jabhat al-Nusra. Should the United States continue to funnel weapons through Baghdad to Kurdish and Sunni factions as opposed to arming them separately? I think yes for now. We have to reinforce governance where it exists, and the governance where it exists today still is centered in Baghdad.

Should the United States increase the number of U.S. troops on the ground in Iraq, and this is where I disagree with my colleague Fred. Moderately increasing the number of troops may improve our operational outcomes, but it will not lead to the destruction of ISIS. We put 150,000 Americans on the ground before. We are talking about a tenth of that now. And I don't believe that this is going to have a decisive outcome because I don't believe that it is sustainable. A mini-surge can push ISIS into a box, a smaller box, but it will still have a box. And having that box is what matters.

Our decade of war against ISIS has not produced a decisive outcome in large measure because our strategy and commitment has been inconsistent. To be successful in the next decade, we must have a clear, consistent, and sustainable strategy. The only good news is that jihadi organizations have a long track record of self-destruction and ISIS is laying the seeds of insurgency against it as we speak with its attacks on Sunnis, its fighting against other Syrian rebel groups. Over time they will collapse, but in order to produce that, we need to have a sustainable strategy rather than an intermittent one that reduces our credibility further in the region.

Mr. WILSON. Thank you very much, Mr. Fishman.

[The prepared statement of Mr. Fishman can be found in the Appendix on page 70.]

Mr. WILSON. And I thank each of you. And Mr. Eisenstadt, you referenced it, and for each person I would be interested in your response beginning with Ms. Robinson about ISIL/Daesh being successful in building a global propaganda campaign to recruit foreign supporters from around the world, reinforcing its battlefield successes and creating an aura of military invincibility.

Why has this global campaign been so effective, appealing to such a broad target audience worldwide, and what approaches should the Pentagon consider to counteract this campaign and reduce the appeal of potential recruits and supporters who can be trained overseas to return home and attack American families? Ms. Robinson.

Ms. ROBINSON. Chairman Wilson, thank you. The brand of ISIL I think is so potent because they have been so enormously successful on the battlefield. They are tactically proficient and far more formidable than what U.S. forces faced when we were there. It is just an order of magnitude different. They are very adept at shifting between maneuvering guerilla warfare, launching new and diversionary attacks, evolving new tactics, and as you know, they trumpet their successes globally, which has drawn new recruits and affiliates.

So that engine, I wish I could agree with Brian, but I think that it doesn't, as I see it, contain the seeds of its own demise. It is going to have to be stopped. And the information warfare I think has to be conducted with Muslim voices indigenous and worldwide. I just do not see the U.S. being effective in the lead.

Now, General Terry, who is the Combined Joint Task Force commander, had been trying for months to get an Arab spokesman for that coalition. I think that is one of those unfortunate things. You wonder, why aren't people stepping up? There is now, I think the co-lead by UAE [United Arab Emirates] for the counter-messaging bin of activities, but I think that the actual content of the message needs to be looked at. And to me, there is no more effective message than one delivered by a disaffected former ISIL fighter.

And I think we have got to get those voices, and those of the families of the ISIL fighters who have died, and what they have been lost to this way of life. And I just think we are far less adept at energizing that kind of messaging, although I would like to note, that the incoming two-star in Baghdad, General Richard Clark, is very key. He has honed in on the media and information aspect of this. Thank you.

Mr. WILSON. Thank you.

Mr. EISENSTADT. Yeah, I would agree with what Ms. Robinson said. And I would just kind of reinforce the point that nothing succeeds like success. And that is a major factor for their appeal. And conversely, I think the most important way to discredit the appeal of their ideology is by military defeat, as Brian said also. You know, if they are not holding terrain, if there is no caliphate, there is no Islamic utopia, it is a lot less appealing as an idea.

I would also, you know, mention, and this is a topic which I'm actually starting to do a lot of thought about, so I don't have a comprehensive, you know, answer to you, but it seems to me that a lot of at least in the public, a lot of the government's—the administration's emphasis has been on countering their religious ideology, and trying to get Muslim voices to discredit it. And as I pointed out in my, you know, remarks, by and large, most supporters of ISIS don't really care what mainstream clerics think about them. They have their own clerics, and they believe that all of these other mainstream clerics are part of the problem.

So I think, I get the sense that perhaps we are pushing, you know, on a locked door. That's not the way to go, by—you know, we can affect things around the edges by trying to counter their ideology and trying to discredit it, but I'm not sure that's the right way to go.

In addition we have to recognize that in this fight, the government is not the most flexible and effective actor. And what we need is to partner with the private sector. We need a troll army of people online who we could provide information to, what the, you know, Combatting Terrorism Center at West Point used to do, publishing captured documents which provide insights into how ISIS functions and the way of how it is to live under ISIS control. So that millions of people online who are Muslims and who object to their message can use the information to fight them.

And then the final point I would just say, we also need a counter narrative because you can't fight something with nothing. And people are flocking to ISIS because it fills a role in terms of their identity, in terms of providing them with meaning in life, and we need to be able to provide, or our allies probably more to the point, need to be able to provide a counter narrative which maybe speaks about inclusiveness, and tolerance, and the like.

Again, these are half-formed ideas, but I think this gives us some vectors for, you know, how to think about this so——

Mr. WILSON. Thank you very much. Dr. Kagan.

Dr. KAGAN. I will be very brief. We don't have a narrative problem. We have a reality problem. And we can talk narrative from hell to breakfast, but the reality is that we are losing and they are winning. And as long as that's the case, there is no narrative that's going to affect the situation very much.

Mr. WILSON. Thank you. Mr. Fishman.

Mr. FISHMAN. I agree very much with that. It is not the—we talk too much about their proficiency with social media, the issue is that their message right now is one of victory. And that's one that people can get behind. The one thing that I would say about what is a credible voice, I agree very much with what Linda said about former fighters.

One of the distinguishing factors at an ideological level of ISIS from Al Qaeda, is that for them authority, ideological and messaging authority, comes from your proximity to a fight, to being in battle. Where Al Qaeda used to point to scholars that would sit around and write things, those of us in think tanks might like that but, you know, but for ISIS, the only thing that gives you ideological authority is being on the battlefield. And so if you are going to push back on them at an ideological level it is going to have to come from somebody with experience in the field.

Mr. WILSON. Well, thank you very much. And I share your concerns that we need to have, Dr. Kagan, an example of success, to— but at the same time, I'm grateful that the House did pass in the Fiscal Year 2016 National Defense Authorization Act [NDAA] authority for the Department to carry out a pilot program to counteract the propaganda campaigns. And I appreciate the concept of a former ISIL supporter and/or family members of deceased ISIL supporters to carry out a campaign to counteract propaganda.

And this provision we hope to be carrying through conference so the Pentagon has the ability to counter Daesh. It is my view that in a bipartisan manner here, that we understand the threat of jihadists who proclaim death to America, death to Israel. And I now proceed to Mr. Veasey.

Mr. VEASEY. Thank you, Mr. Chairman, and I think I have a question that any of the panelists here can answer. And I know we have talked before about how ISIL is very in tune to what is going on here culturally, you know, from the media, particularly social media.

And they also have, I'm sure have seen news reports on the question about what to do about ISIL. What do you think that the ISIL leadership is thinking as far as their biggest fear is concerned? Do you think it's, you know, more air strikes from America? That we would eventually put troops on the ground? That we would arm factions within their so-called caliphate? What is the thing that makes ISIL fear the most?

Dr. KAGAN. I think that it's been very clear that the thing they fear the most is what happened to them that defeated them before, which is the Awakening. And they most fear that the populations

14

that they live amongst will turn against them and will be supported against them. And I think they feared to some extent that we will assist that, but they have been carrying out a ruthless campaign of assassinations, as Brian pointed out, for many, many years now, precisely to forestall that option. Because I think that is the one that they regard as most permanently damaging and threatening to them.

Mr. VEASEY. In regards to that, you know, when they come into an area and they want to set up this caliphate, they want to do it, obviously, with Sunni Muslims. With so many Sunni Muslims being very distrustful of Shia Muslims, particularly in Iraq, how do you build the support for the people that they are in control of if you were to try to form some sort of a coalition, or arm them, or what have you, how can you—with that Sunni versus Shia element going on there, how can you make something like that real and sustainable?

Dr. KAGAN. Congressman, I think you really put your finger on what is in many respects the most important issue here, which is that we have, as Brian and my other colleagues have said, we have a sectarian war throughout the region and it is actually going global. And that sectarian war is in my opinion the largest, most powerful, long-term driver of mobilization and radicalization in both of these communities.

As long as that sectarian war continues to rage, it is going to be very, very difficult to defeat ISIS, or Al Qaeda, or get Iranian-backed militias in the box or anything like that. And so that's one of the reasons why the notion of containment fails completely because containment retains this escalating sectarian civil war which has exactly the consequences that you described.

Mr. EISENSTADT. I would just jump in one other thing that we just have to remember. That we were, as you intimated, part of the last effort to foment an uprising against ISIL's predecessor. And we, as a result of the past experience where we promised them, if you fight with us, and eventually the Iraqi Government against Al Qaeda, we will look after you, and we didn't.

So we have—there's a problem with the credibility of the Iraqi Government and there is a problem with our credibility which will make it much harder to replicate the past success. In addition, there are various other factors that, you know, kind of play into the mix now that we just don't have a large presence on the ground the way we did in 2007 and after in order to actually change the psychological dynamic in the way that we need to in order to get the people, you know, people to rise up against an adversary or right now the Islamic State who is so vicious and cruel.

Ms. ROBINSON. May I just add briefly, I think that it is important to recognize that Prime Minister Abadi has made more overtures to the Sunni community, certainly, than his predecessor did. And I think that there is room for, in Iraq, diplomatic outreach to try to support that and try to build links with the Shia majority with the idea of helping to encourage them that ultimately their interests can be served by these non-military pathways to resolution. For example, really laying out a roadmap for the decentralization of Iraq because I think that is ultimately the only way the country is going to hold together.

I think also regionally, I would like to note Saudi Arabia finally opened its embassy in Baghdad that could provide a first step to build upon building relations between and contacts between Iraq and the Gulf States. But I think it's very important that Abadi do that outreach because, obviously, the Gulf States are quite concerned about the reality of Iraq's closeness to Iran.

Mr. VEASEY. Very briefly, with the last few seconds that I have, the White House's new hostage policy. How do you think that ISIL will view that?

Mr. FISHMAN. I don't think it's going to impact their decision making very much at all, to be honest. I don't think they see that as their primary fundraising mechanism. Those people, as we know too well, are more valuable to ISIS as sort of propaganda tools than anything else.

Mr. VEASEY. Thank you. Thank you, Mr. Chairman.

Mr. WILSON. Thank you very much, Mr. Veasey. And as you cited, a sectarian war and conflict, I had the opportunity this year to meet with a descendant of the Prophet Muhammad who explained to me that the sectarian war has been ongoing for 1,400 years.

We now proceed to Sheriff Nugent.

Mr. NUGENT. Thank you, Mr. Chairman, and I think that's the biggest problem that you hit on is that sectarian portion of it. But let's talk about the Kurds for a moment. They have had some great success. And you talked about, you know, the arms that we are supplying the Iraqis that have to flow through the central government to the Kurds and we saw that that was not actually working very well. But supposedly, it is working better today.

And I understand the reason for that, but aren't we sort of chasing our tail on this because we think that, you know, we are going to build some rapport with the Kurds to the central government in Iraq, and they don't feel any allegiance to it, you know, just because to give them some weapons, do you really think that narrative is going to change the outcome as it relates to the Kurds and Iraqi state itself?

Dr. KAGAN. Congressman, I think that it's—what would really change the dynamic is if we started treating Kurdistan as an independent state, and sending weapons directly to Kurdistan. I think the notion—we are not binding them to Baghdad by sending weapons through Baghdad, but we would be making a positive statement that we are effectively treating them as independent if we started sending weapons directly to Kurdistan.

And I think that we really need to be careful of overestimating what the Kurds' capabilities actually are. And geography is a problem here because the Kurds are not going to clear Anbar. They are just not. And in point of fact, I actually believe that if you saw Kurdish forces push into Mosul and push into Al Diwaniyah province, you would start and we are beginning to see little indicators of this, an ethnic war as the Arabs in those regions push back against what they would perceive to be Kurdish encroachment on their territory and that would be overlaid on a sectarian war.

So I think we really need to be careful. I'm all about helping the Kurds defend Kurdistan——

Mr. NUGENT. Right.

Dr. KAGAN [continuing]. I think we can do that, but I think we need to avoid as some people are trying—seeing Kurds as the solution to this problem.

Mr. NUGENT. Yeah. I don't think they are either. The Deputy Secretary of State recently was spouting numbers almost, you know, like in Vietnam, where we had 10,000 casualties, we have, you know, eliminated 6,000 pieces of equipment. What does that mean? I mean, is there any value in stating that, because that's not an indicator of winning. It's just an indicator that we killed people, and we demolished stuff.

Mr. EISENSTADT. Yeah, I, you know, body counts are, as we know from our Vietnam experience, very deceiving and very dangerous. I will just say two points: First, it only matters if they have a finite manpower pool, and we need to know are they able to replace the people being killed or are they recruiting people faster than you are losing them. And I will leave it at that. That's, I think, the——

Mr. NUGENT. Well, let me ask you this, your opinion. Has ISIL been degraded since August of last year since we started this campaign or have they gotten stronger?

Mr. EISENSTADT. Well, yeah, let me just complete my thought on that one. Attrition matters to the degree that they are over-extended, and further overextending them might make them vulnerable to internal uprisings or further attacks along the borders of the areas they control. So I think attrition is not irrelevant, but it's dangerous as a metric that stands alone.

In terms of their capabilities, look, there have been areas they have been rolled back, and there are areas that they have pushed back successfully. So I think—and they have shown an ability to move their forces from Syria to Iraq, and back again.

So they overall, they have been attrited, but their capabilities remain overall relatively robust to the degree that they are able to maintain offensives and continue to gain ground in areas that are important for them. I don't think you could say that they have lost ground except for Tikrit which was I think important on a certain level symbolically, that they have lost ground in any areas that were critical for them. And they gained the provincial capital of Anbar which was an important psychological gain for them. And Palmyra is, too, important—in the context of Syria is very important.

Mr. FISHMAN. I think one of the things to keep in mind about ISIS, or ISIL, is that it, to maintain function, to be a functional organization it needs to stay on offense. It needs to have that message of fighting to get recruits, to keep people motivated. It is not going to do a good job hunkering down and defending a specific territory. And I think that you see that in some of the ways it has exposed itself and I would argue that, you know, they are probably sitting around in a room saying, look, we have expanded in some places. We have lost in others. You know, does our geographic footprint need to fundamentally change? Did we try to take the right places? You know, where can we hunker down? Where can we actually be more secure? And I don't think they know that.

My expectation is that they will be, the territory they control will contract by the end of 2015. It will still be a very viable organization, and one that is extremely resilient going forward, but I expect they will contract more this year.

Mr. NUGENT. Mr. Chairman, I appreciate it and I yield back.

Mr. WILSON. Thank you, Mr. Nugent. We now proceed to Mr. Zinke.

Mr. ZINKE. Thank you, Mr. Chairman. I agree with your assessment of the Kurds, having followed the Kurds. I don't think they are going to look at Mosul primarily because you have about 500,000 refugees. If they attempted, the refugees can't go north, they can't go south. The only way they could go is in Kurd-held territory. I don't think they want that or could afford that.

I also agree with your assessment on Syria; until we figure out what we are going to do with Syria, whether we are going to arm the Syrian Free Army, having the desert as an area of sanctuary to a degree with ISIS is problematic.

But what I'm not hearing is Iran, Persia. And the influence in now eastern Iraq. Reports I think are validated that you have the Badr Army now moving to what is, in my experience was never more than about 7,000, the Shia militia seems to be operating at now 30 to 40,000 at full strength, seem to be either closely coordinated or directly controlled by Iran. You have senior military leadership embedded.

And so my question is, and this has been a change of sea for me, because I looked at Iraq and thought there are multiple opportunities for us to check ISIS. And we have passed many of those. And now if we enter and we cede territory from ISIS, and if the result is simply for a Shia militia, which is to a degree controlled by Iran, to now if we are ceding territory from ISIS and simply having that territory being filled by Iran, and their continuing influence in Iraq, then what's the point? Do you share a concern, Dr. Kagan, about Iran's seem to be expanding influence particularly in eastern Iraq and the effects it has with disenfranchising further the Sunni population?

Dr. KAGAN. Absolutely. And it is not just eastern Iraq, it is Baghdad, and it is Anbar, and it is throughout Iraq. I think that there is a lot of complexity among the Shia militias that we're seeing on the ground and I think it is important not to lump them all together, not that you did.

By the way, Badr just basically seized the governorship of Diyala Province which is going to be problematic from the standpoint of National Guard law, among many other things. But you have Badr, and you have Kata'ib Hezbollah [KH], which are basically arms of the Quds Force in my assessment and are basically commanded by Soleimani.

You have Asa'ib Ahl al-Haq [AAH], which is not quite there, but close, but then you have popular mobilization forces that actually responded to Grand Ayatollah Sistani's call, and I don't believe that all of those are controlled by Badr, or KH, or AAH. And I do believe that there is a possibility that those forces, some of those forces could be integrated into the ISF, and are less under the Iranian control. I think the issue is, if we assess and I do agree with Linda Robinson that Prime Minister Abadi is much better than his predecessor, who was a major driver of sectarian conflict. And I think that the Prime Minister really actually has the right goals in mind.

Mr. ZINKE. We agree on that.

Dr. KAGAN. But I think he is being pushed hard by radical Shia militias and by Iranian advisors in a sectarian direction. And I think that it is very important that we offer him enough of an alternative, and that we overcome or try to overcome the military gap that Mike Eisenstadt pointed out, to let him—to give him an opportunity to try to unwind these militias from control of his state because he is not really sovereign in even what he controls, as long as Soleimani is commanding armed forces in his territory.

Mr. ZINKE. And Ms. Robinson, I agree with much of your assessment as well. How do you see the Iranian influence being checked and pushed out of the territory of Iraq? Because I think that's a core issue that as you continue the Iranian influence, how is it that we are going to push them back across in Iranian territory rather than territory of Iraq? Is it possible?

Ms. ROBINSON. Well, I would like to start by quoting my esteemed friend Ambassador Ryan Crocker who said, Iran is not going to leave the borders of Iraq. It is always going to be a neighbor of Iraq. So it is a long-term issue, and I don't think we can wave a wand and make Iran or Iranian influence go away.

But I think the critical question for the U.S. is, are we going to cede Iraq to Iranian influence or are we going to get in there and play the influence game? And I think that includes a much more robust outreach to a whole range of Shia forces. And I appreciate what Fred said, and also your comment, the Shia mosaic is quite complex. There are the standing, longstanding Shia militias we have already mentioned, but also new splinter groups that are supposedly less anti-American. They might be more receptive to outreach, and then these volunteers that came forward because Ayatollah Sistani said, come and defend your country.

And he, of course, is, I think, a main critical figure so long as he is still alive to try to weave that, find that path between Iranian dominance and Shia-Iraqi nationalism, which is not dead, but much mitigated. So I think it is a long-term project, but really, we have to be, and it is part of a political line of effort that I think we have to open up and encourage our diplomats to be part of. Again, citing my friend Ryan Crocker who was fully engaged in that. Thank you.

Mr. ZINKE. Thank you. And thank you all for being here.

And, Mr. Chairman, I yield back.

Mr. WILSON. Thank you very much, Mr. Zinke. Thank you for your service here and thank you for your service as a Navy SEAL.

I will now proceed to the vice chairman of the subcommittee, Trent Franks of Arizona.

Mr. FRANKS. Well, thank you, Mr. Chairman. And thank all of you for being here. I have to suggest I am going to try to probably piggyback off of a couple of comments that have already been made, starting with the Kurdish issue. Last week during the HASC [House Armed Services Committee] hearing, I questioned Secretary of Defense Carter on the administration's strategy on ISIS, and, of course, you know, many of us know that even though that Dr. Kagan is correct about the Kurdish not being able to do—they are certainly limited, but they have been a bright spot in this situation, and we did pass an amendment in the full committee here to give direct support to the Kurds for that reason alone.

But after the Secretary himself responded in steadfast agreement that the Kurds were making progress, then the State Department, the Defense Department, and the U.S. Ambassador to Iraq have derailed Senator Joni Ernst's efforts to do the same on the Senate floor last week with a very intense lobbying effort. And to quote a senior administration official, this—this is the quote, it says, ''the U.S. gives weapons directly only to the Iraqi Government and to the Iraqi Security Forces, but the lines between them and the militias are blurry. U.S. weapons often fall into the hands of militias like Iraqi Hezbollah. There is no real command and control from the central government.''

And that seems to underscore what I am saying here, this bank shot that the administration tries to do. Using the Iraqi central government as the distribution mechanism doesn't seem to be working very well.

Do you think—and then, Dr. Kagan, I will ask for a quick answer, because I am hoping to get one more question in. Do you think that it is sound policy to just kind of hope for the best and hope some of the money will get to the Kurds, or do you think that we need to be more direct in our effort to assist the Kurds and the Peshmerga in doing at least some of the good work that they are doing?

Dr. KAGAN. Sir, I don't think hope is ever a good method——

Mr. FRANKS. Yeah.

Dr. KAGAN [continuing]. But I think this goes beyond hope. And I think that as far as I have been able to hear and follow up on this, the Kurds are largely getting what they need, and I don't think it is a good idea to be providing support directly to Kurdistan.

Mr. FRANKS. Help me understand that. Why not?

Dr. KAGAN. Because the—when you provide direct support to Kurdistan, and I understand and sympathize with the motivations of the committee and the members supporting that.

Mr. FRANKS. Because they are the only ones kicking ISIS' rear.

Dr. KAGAN. Right. But they can only do that up to a point, and the problem is that by supporting the Kurds directly, you are making a statement unintentionally about Kurdish independence and the Kurdish role in——

Mr. FRANKS. Well, I know we wouldn't want to hurt anybody's feelings here, but I guess I am just concerned about that, you know, somebody's got to fight ISIS, and this administration is not doing that.

Dr. KAGAN. I can't disagree with that enough, but the Kurds are not going to be able to do it either, and so we are going to have to find partners in Arab Iraq, and that means that there is a limit to how much we can afford to side with the Kurds and what is after all a——

Mr. FRANKS. Who is a better partner than the Kurds right now?

Dr. KAGAN. Right now we—well, the partner that we need is in the Sunni Arab community, that is the partner that we most need. And the problem is that the more that you support the Kurds in

Ninawa and along the disputed areas and the Kurds push into those areas, the more that we put ourselves against the Sunni Arab community that might otherwise join us in fighting ISIS.

Now, we don't have a strategy that is going to get them to join us fighting ISIS right now and we need to address that, but I am afraid that the Kurdish arming—arming the Kurds directly could be counterproductive.

Mr. FRANKS. Let me switch gears. I would just suggest to you that the Sunnis weren't fighting the ISIS very effectively before, where the Kurdish at least were trying.

We know that the deadline for the P5+1 [United States, Russia, China, France, United Kingdom, plus Germany] nuclear negotiations with Iran is about a week away and this administration seems hellbent on doing a deal no matter what it is, and the only thing it seems to be willing—is possible to get in their way is the intransigence of the Tehran government themselves, that they can't—you know.

So this concern midterm could have implications across the Middle East that is hard to fathom right now, and I—what effects do you see happening of the injection into the Iranian economy of billions of dollars, under such a potential agreement, to sponsor additional terrorism in the region? Do you think that them getting a great deal more money is going to somehow to make this all better?

Dr. KAGAN. The Iranian regime has been extremely clear that it has no intention whatsoever of altering any of its policies in the region or toward the United States, regardless of whether there is a deal. They regard us as an enemy and they intend to continue to pursue efforts to drive us from the region and destroy our allies.

If they receive a significant influx of additional resources, they will put it, among other things, to the purpose of increasing their military and paramilitary capabilities throughout the region and throughout the world.

Mr. FRANKS. Well, I couldn't agree with you more, Dr. Kagan.

And I would just say, Mr. Chairman, that as dangerous as ISIS is, we need to fight them, but we cannot take our eye off of the Iranian nuclear threat. And I yield back.

Mr. WILSON. Thank you, Mr. Franks.

And we now proceed to Mr. Lamborn of Colorado.

Mr. LAMBORN. Thank you, Mr. Chairman, for having this hearing. Thank you all for being here. And I would like to ask you about our targeting of ISIS assets. The New York Times reported on May 26 that, quote, "American officials say that they are not striking significant and obvious Islamic State targets, out of fear that the attacks will accidentally kill civilians, but many Iraqi commanders and some American officers say that exercising such prudence with air strikes is a major reason ISIS has been able to seize vast territory in recent months in Iraq and Syria."

Dr. Kagan, would you agree with that assessment? And is it possible to step up air strikes while still, to the degree possible, preserving civilian lives?

Dr. KAGAN. I think that there is a trade-off between deciding that you are going to have a more effective air campaign and accepting a higher risk of civilian casualties.

I think if your standard for civilian casualties is low, you are probably going to have a very hard time increasing the intensity of the air campaign, especially as long as you are not prepared to put forward air controllers on the ground, which would be something that would mitigate that, but I think that we have too high a standard from the standpoint of collateral damage and civilian casualties. I think that the truth is this is a war. And we always try to minimize collateral damage and civilian casualties, but a standard of effectively zero has, I think, done enormous harm to our ability to prosecute this war with the tools that we have at our disposal.

Mr. LAMBORN. Thank you. And then for any one of you, I am really concerned about Jordan's welfare. They have the direct threat of ISIS wanting to overcome them, and they have the indirect threat of floods of refugees from Syria especially overwhelming their infrastructure and their budget.

What can we do to better help Jordan? What should Jordan be doing to help itself?

Ms. ROBINSON. I am glad you raised that, because I did include mention of Jordan in my written remarks, and I think it is critical. Jordan, of course, does have a very effective and efficient military, police, and intelligence service, but that said, I think the waves of refugees pose a long-term threat, not just a humanitarian issue, but to the political and economic fabric of that country, as well as the surrounding region.

And I think that trying to get more involved with those refugee populations, possibly through international organizations, but to deepen the understanding of what is going on there and help to ensure that they don't become subject to concerted radicalization campaigns or support networks, and to eventually find a disposition for these people, I doubt they are going to go—most of them will go back home, so this poses a very critical long-term threat.

Mr. FISHMAN. Just one thing to add to that. I absolutely agree that we shouldn't expect that they are going to go home, and we should plan that this is—these are not just refugees, these are—many of these people are going to be new citizens essentially of Jordan, but this is a place where many of our Arab allies, I think, also have a responsibility, and we should be leading politically to pull them along. It is a place where they can contribute. Even if they are not going to contribute militarily, this is something where they can contribute, where money matters, and they can offer that.

Mr. LAMBORN. And either Mr. Eisenstadt or Dr. Kagan, anything to add to that?

Dr. KAGAN. I think it is—you are making an excellent point, and I am also very worried about Jordan and the strain that is being put on it. And I would just turn it in a slightly different way, because there are a lot of people in town who are talking about the need to raise an Arab army to fight in Syria and Iraq and the Jordanians should fight and the Saudis should fight and so forth, and you have highlighted one of the reasons why that is not really feasible. The Jordanians, I would not be enthusiastic about calling on the Jordanians to deploy large numbers of their own forces abroad, for a whole bunch of reasons.

Mr. EISENSTADT. And I will just add, you can't worry too much about Jordan, because of its importance vis-a-vis our allies, Saudi, Israel, but that said, keep in mind they have been dealing with the problem of refugees for well over a decade now, or actually even longer, and their resilience and their ability to do so is remarkable, but that said, we can't take them for granted, they are absolutely a critical ally of ours. And we are doing things. They get financial aid, they get military assistance. I can't say whether we should be doing more or not, but I think we are focused on that issue.

Mr. LAMBORN. Well, and you probably know in the NDAA, which is going to be going to conference, we just voted on with the Senate, I think we put in 300-plus million dollars of very good military aid for Jordan.

Thank you for being here.

Mr. WILSON. Thank you very much, Mr. Lamborn.

And we now—we have been joined by Congresswoman Martha McSally, of Arizona, the very first female air combat pilot to serve in Congress.

Congresswoman McSally.

Ms. MCSALLY. Thank you, Mr. Chairman. And thank you. I am not on this committee, but I wanted to join this. I appreciate the testimony and your perspectives. I know there is a lot of talk about specifically the strategy about ISIS and I know you have—in the discussions on Iran talked a little bit more about the regional dynamic. A big concern that I have is the incoherence of a strategy in the region especially vis-a-vis Iran, the elephant in the room.

We have got—we are focusing a lot on ISIS, which is important, but we are kind of looking through a soda straw without realizing some of the dynamics with our Sunni allies are related to the incoherence and the inconsistencies in how we are dealing with Iran, on the one hand doing everything we can to get to a nuclear weapon, on the other hand allowing them—you know, Soleimani to be the ground force commander while we are providing the air forces in Tikrit, and vis-a-vis what we are doing in Yemen.

I mean, it is totally incoherent. So I would like to get your perspectives on that incoherence and what we could be doing better regionally to address not just ISIS, but also this larger state sponsor of terror on the globe, which is Iran, and then I want to follow up with some discussion on the air campaign.

Mr. EISENSTADT. Yeah. If I could just start off by saying, first of all, we will never be able to iron out all the contradictions in our policies. There are just way too many moving pieces in this part of the world, and we will never be able to square the circle. But that said, I would argue that just as during the Cold War, while negotiating arms control deals with the Soviet Union, we pushed back against Soviet aggression and proxy activities around the world. We should be doing more in that regard with Iran.

I am fully supportive of trying to put the relationship between the United States and Iran on a more normal basis while still acting to advance our interests and to defend the interests of our allies, which means doing more things in Syria with regard to the opposition there, doing things like we are doing, we are doing, to the credit of the administration, with regard to interdicting arms shipments to the Houthis in Yemen and some of the things we are doing in Iraq, but we needed to have been a lot more forceful than we have.

And some of the things that the spokesperson of the administration has stated in public have sent the wrong signal in terms of acquiescing to what is seen in the region as Iran's attempts to establish a modern-day empire.

So we need to—it is a matter of finessing or striking the right balance in our policy, and we have not hit the right balance. There is more we could do.

Ms. MCSALLY. All right. Dr. Kagan, any thoughts on that or——

Dr. KAGAN. I really want to second what Mike said and also what Brian said earlier. Absolutely, once you talk to one's enemies, you can negotiate with your enemy, you don't have to surrender every other interest that you have while negotiating with your enemy, and we should be pushing back.

And what Brian said earlier was really, really important. We have to support opposition in Syria against Assad, otherwise, we have no meaningful opposition in Syria to support.

Ms. MCSALLY. Exactly. Thank you. Now, turning to the military strategy against ISIS, I was critical last week to the Secretary of Defense and to the chairman related to our air campaign. And I think we have got this false choice, really, narrative in the media: it is either an air campaign that seems to not be working or it is hundreds of thousands of boots on the ground.

And the reality is it seems like we are stuck in a counterinsurgency mind-set that we have been mired in over the last 14 years, and we are forgetting that we have vital national interests in stopping ISIS that are separate and distinct from Iraq's interests in the region and what we are trying to get them to do.

And so I feel very frustrated that we are not using airpower, as an airman, to the extent that we can use it, where we minimize civilian casualties, but we hit the targets that are legitimate in order to take out the command and control, the logistics, the leadership, everything it takes for ISIS to be able to be continuing to have the momentum.

So it is very frustrating. And I have heard and read your testimony. I believe we need more intelligence, more JTACs, we need to be using airpower in a stronger way, we need to raise the bar. To save one civilian casualty, but then allow ISIS to murder thousands of people on the ground is absolutely contradictory. We have got to be able to gain the momentum and use airpower, and I just want your perspectives on that.

Dr. KAGAN. Well, I couldn't agree with you more. And I find it baffling that ISIS has been able to maneuver mechanized forces around this battlefield in airspace—while we control the airspace.

Ms. MCSALLY. Exactly.

Dr. KAGAN. We have an entire military designed to prevent people from doing that——

Ms. MCSALLY. Exactly.

Dr. KAGAN [continuing]. So we certainly can, and we—as you say, we certainly can do it with minimum casualties and we can do it without putting 150,000 thousand troops on the ground also, and we should do it.

Ms. MCSALLY. Exactly. Thank you.

Mr. EISENSTADT. If I could just add, my understanding is that we have until recently perhaps had most of our ISR in Afghanistan to support the drawdown there, and now I guess—and if you look at the trend lines of ISR sorties in Iraq and Syria, they are trending up.

So there is a—I suspect there is—some of that assets are being now redeployed to the fight there to support it, but that said, probably need more and we probably need to be more aggressive with our air strikes, and as Fred and others have said, strike a different balance with regard to the trade-offs with regard to our concern to collateral damage and the need to consistently be pushing ISIS back, and show that momentum has changed.

Ms. MCSALLY. And we can gain the space then, therefore, for the political solution, but if we are letting them get the momentum because we are not using our elements of military power that we have in the way that is best used, then we are surrendering.

Mr. EISENSTADT. Well, that is a critical point, because every day Sunnis are making life and death calculations about which side do they throw their support behind. And if they see that—if they believe that after rising up against ISIS, 6 months from now ISIL will be back——

Ms. MCSALLY. Yes.

Mr. EISENSTADT [continuing]. Because of our fecklessness——

Ms. MCSALLY. Exactly.

Mr. EISENSTADT [continuing]. They are not going to do that, and therefore, we need—there needs to be a consistent perception of progress being made, and we can't afford to allow them to claw back—ISIL to claw back territory that has been lost—or that was not under their control.

Ms. MCSALLY. Great. Thank you. My time has long expired. Thank you, Mr. Chairman, for letting me join the committee hearing today.

Mr. WILSON. And thank you, Ms. McSally, for your insight and thank you for joining us today on the subcommittee.

And I want to thank each of you. This has really been very helpful, and each one of you have had points that we need to be concerned.

And I do have one request of Dr. Kagan. Two years ago you provided an extraordinary map indicating the spread of Al Qaeda and its affiliates across North Africa, Central Africa, and the Middle East, Central Asia. And for the benefit of our subcommittee members, if you could provide, if you do have, and I hope you do, an update of that map, it was extraordinarily helpful as I was explaining to my constituents the threats that we are facing from that region.

If there is no further, we are adjourned.

[Whereupon, at 3:48 p.m., the subcommittee was adjourned.]

APPENDIX

June 24, 2015

PREPARED STATEMENTS SUBMITTED FOR THE RECORD

JUNE 24, 2015

Chairman Wilson Opening Statement
Hearing
"The Counterterrorism Strategy Against the Islamic State of Iraq and the Levant (ISIL): Are We on the Right Path?"
24 June 2015

Ladies and gentlemen, I call this hearing of the Emerging Threats and Capabilities subcommittee of the House Armed Services Committee to order.

I am pleased to welcome everyone here today for this very important hearing on the counterterrorism strategy against the Islamic State of Iraq and the Levant. ISIL – or DAASH – continues to spread and create instability throughout the Middle East, northern Africa and Asia. Their propaganda and insidious campaign of influence extends globally, manipulating and recruiting young men and women who are willing to die for DAASH.

The trajectory we are on is not promising. The President himself has acknowledged that we do not yet have a complete strategy to combat ISIL. Defense Secretary Carter has acknowledged that the military is reviewing how to increase the effectiveness of our campaign, and that an additional 450 troops would deploy to Iraq to expand the advise and assist mission.

When I last visited Iraq in February of this year along with Representatives Seth Moulton, Elise Stefanik and Brad Ashford, there was talk that the Iraqi Army would begin taking back Mosul by the summer.

Today, sadly, we see that this is not the case.

While often characterized as a terrorist organization, ISIL fights and behaves like an army. They remain well funded and resourced. And as we saw recently in Ramadi, they do not necessarily need overwhelming numbers to win on the battlefield; only an ability to strike fear in the hearts of those they encounter.

Today, we seek answers to very simple but serious questions of national importance:

First, are we on the right path to defeat ISIL?

Second, what problems exist with our current counterterrorism strategy?

And lastly, what other actions could we take to counter this evolving national security threat?

We will not answer all of these questions today. But what will be certain is the fact that it will take <u>years</u> to render ISIL ineffective. Because of that, we cannot ignore the pressure of declining defense budgets and the looming shadow of Defense Sequestration. As we examine our strategy against ISIL, we must remind ourselves that if Defense Sequestration continues, we will truly be fighting this threat with one hand tied behind our back.

We are fortunate today to have before us a panel of expert witnesses. They are:

- Ms. Linda Robinson, a Senior International Policy Analyst with the RAND Corporation;
- Mr. Michael Eisenstadt , the Director of the Military and Security Studies Program at the Washington Institute for Near East Policy
- Dr. Fred Kagan, the Director of the Critical Threats Project at the American Enterprise Institute; and
- Mr. Brian Fishman, a Counterterrorism Research Fellow with the International Studies Program at the New America Foundation

I'd like to turn now to my friend, Mr. Jim Langevin from Rhode Island, for any comments he'd like to make.

An Assessment of the Counter-ISIL Campaign

One Year after Mosul

Linda Robinson

RAND Office of External Affairs

CT-435

June 2015

Testimony presented before the House Armed Services Committee, Subcommittee on Emerging Threats and Capabilities on June 24, 2015

32

Published 2015 by the RAND Corporation
1776 Main Street, P.O. Box 2138, Santa Monica, CA 90407-2138
1200 South Hayes Street, Arlington, VA 22202-5050
4570 Fifth Avenue, Suite 600, Pittsburgh, PA 15213-2665
RAND URL: http://www.rand.org/
To order RAND documents or to obtain additional information, contact
Distribution Services: Telephone: (310) 451-7002;
Email: order@rand.org

Linda Robinson[1]
The RAND Corporation

An Assessment of the Counter-ISIL Campaign
One Year after Mosul[2]

Before the Committee on Armed Services
Subcommittee on Emerging Threats and Capabilities
House of Representatives

June 24, 2015

Chairman Wilson, Ranking Member Langevin, and members of the subcommittee: Thank you for the opportunity to testify again before this important subcommittee of the HASC. I returned on May 31 from a ten-day trip to Iraq and Jordan, which is my second research trip to the region this year. I visited many of the U.S., coalition and Iraqi commands and operations centers, and met with civilian and military leaders, officials, and troops at various echelons.

I will summarize my observations on the counter-ISIL military line of operations. Second, I will offer a few observations about the overall synchronization of the campaign and the political line of effort. I will finish with my assessment of the options for U.S. policy and the questions this committee is asking after one year of this campaign, namely:

1. Does the United States have the right strategy? Can ISIL be defeated and destroyed through a partnered approach? Are alternative strategies more promising?

2. Are the ways and means being applied under the current strategy adequate?

Assessment of ISIL

There is now, among U.S. and coalition officers, a very keen appreciation for the capabilities of the Islamic State, also known as ISIL or ISIS. The group has proven to be resilient, agile, and adaptive. Despite losses that approximate half of their estimated fighting force since the U.S. airstrikes began in August 2014, ISIL fighters have dug into Mosul, captured Ramadi, are still

---

[1] The opinions and conclusions expressed in this testimony are the author's alone and should not be interpreted as representing those of RAND or any of the sponsors of its research. This product is part of the RAND Corporation testimony series. RAND testimonies record testimony presented by RAND associates to federal, state, or local legislative committees; government-appointed commissions and panels; and private review and oversight bodies. The RAND Corporation is a nonprofit research organization providing objective analysis and effective solutions that address the challenges facing the public and private sectors around the world. RAND's publications do not necessarily reflect the opinions of its research clients and sponsors.
[2] This testimony is available for free download at http://www.rand.org/pubs/testimonies/CT435.html.

fighting at Baiji, and are expected to re-attack areas such as Tikrit and Diyala.[3] They have been able to resupply both fighters and materiel through internal lines running into Syria and externally through Turkey. They are tactically proficient; small squads can stop a company or more with a variety of weapons, improvised explosive devices (IEDs), and evolving tactics. They have replaced leaders, moved between maneuver and guerrilla warfare as circumstances dictate, and launched new or diversionary attacks to maintain momentum. They trumpet their successes globally, which brings them recruits and affiliates. While ISIL just faced a setback on the Turkish border that could prove important (i.e., the capture of Tel Abyad), it has maintained and expanded its territory in Syria.

Assessment of Counter-ISIL Forces

The anti-ISIL forces on the ground are characterized by 1) limited capability, 2) varying intentions, and 3) an overall lack of coordination. A detailed analysis of each group follows.

- First, the Iraqi Security Forces (ISF) are not at present an effective force able to serve as the main fighting element. According to the U.S. Embassy's Office of Security Cooperation, on paper, Iraq has an army of 14 divisions, one armored, three mechanized, and ten infantry. The United States does not have a detailed grasp of how many forces are actually present for duty, but estimates run about 50 percent less than on paper. Some 40,000–70,000 of those unfilled positions are called "ghost soldiers," for whom salaries are paid; these funds either go into officers' pockets or are used to pay for legitimate unfunded needs. As Secretary Carter noted in this committee's full hearing last week, units showed up for the U.S. and coalition training far from fully manned: The units were 40–70 percent below the brigade's 2,750 manning profile, and many officers did not show either. While there are good officers, and some poor officers have been fired, many substandard officers remain on the job, and some serve in critical positions.

    - In addition to questions about manning, the United States does not know exactly what equipment, weapons, and ammunition our Iraqi partners have, because we

---

[3] In an interview with French radio after a coalition meeting in Paris, Deputy Secretary of State Anthony Blinken said that more than 10,000 ISIL fighters had been killed ("U.S. says 10,000 Islamic State Militants Killed in Nine-Month Campaign," Reuters, June 3, 2015). At an Air Force Association breakfast, General Hawk Carlisle, the commander of the Air Combat Command, stated that 13,000 ISIL fighters have been killed (Sarah Caspari, "Air Force: ISIS Selfie Led to Its Headquarters Destruction," *Christian Science Monitor*, June 5, 2015). Director of National Intelligence James Clapper testified on February 26, 2015, to Congress that U.S. intelligence estimated ISIL fighters at 20,000 to 32,000 ("Hearing to Receive Testimony on Worldwide Threats," Stenographic Transcript Before the Committee on Armed Services, Washington, D.C., February 26, 2015, available at: http://www.armed-services.senate.gov/imo/media/doc/15-18%20-%202-26-15.pdf).

do not have regular access to their depots and they lack good accountability systems. I will say more about the U.S. and coalition equipping effort below, but the basic picture is this: The depots are full of ammunition and small arms, but heavy weapons and armored vehicles are scarce. Prime Minister Abadi recently noted that 2,300 high mobility military vehicles (HMMVs) were taken by ISIL after troops fled Mosul last year, and some of those are now used as powerful bombs.[4] The United States has just announced that 35 mine-resistant ambush protected vehicles with mine-rollers are ready for delivery to Iraq, but the U.S. command urged that they be reserved for use in Mosul.

– More than 40 percent of the ISF is assigned to the Baghdad operations command, in a reflection of both the government's priority of defending the capital and its assessment that ISIL can indeed threaten it. A third rationale was mentioned, which is the desire for balance so that Ministry of Interior forces are not the only guns in the city. Finally, the Baghdad Operations Command has recently been assigned responsibility for retaking parts of eastern Anbar from ISIL. Another significant portion of the ISF is devoted to Diyala and the Shia provinces to the south.

• Second, the Counter-Terrorism Service (CTS) is Iraq's special operations element. I note that the Secretary of Defense amended his remark about the ISF lacking a will to fight, and I'd like to underscore this amendment by noting the following: Since December 2013, the CTS has been deployed in every major battle. It has suffered 2,636 casualties as of last month, which reduced its fighting force to somewhere between 6,000 to 7,000 troops from its authorized level of 11,000.[5] I talked to the CTS commander, General Kenani, about this operational tempo; he said it was too high, but he has no choice but to comply when the Prime Minister orders troops deployed. The problem is that CTS has been inadequately supported by other forces. He also noted that putting a small number of forces out in fixed positions is not the way this force was intended to be used. The CTS forces were pinned down in Baiji's oil refinery for months without relief and watched more than two dozen of their wounded comrades die. They are still fighting there. This experience probably influenced their decision to withdraw from Ramadi. While CTS was used for sectarian ends under Prime Minister Maliki, it seems to have maintained a nonsectarian recruiting policy and ethos. In my meeting with him, Kenani, a Shia,

---

[4] Alexander Smith, "Iraq PM Says Forces Lost 2,300 HMMVs Last Year to ISIS," nbcnews.com, June 1, 2015, available at: http://www.nbcnews.com/storyline/isis-terror/iraqi-prime-minister-haider-al-abadi-says-his-forces-lost-n367596.
[5] Counter-Terrorism Service records.

introduced me to his Sunni deputy, as well as a Christian staff member. He said that the belief that "We are all Iraqis first" was a central criterion for membership in the unit.

- CTS is under great stress. A number of U.S. Special Operations Forces (SOF) advisers believe that CTS could crumble under the strain, if the way in which its forces are employed and supported does not change. There are frictions between CTS and the Ministry of Defense, partly because these are separate organizations. Parliament has not provided CTS its own separate budget, so its funding has been precarious. CTS's current urgent needs are armored HMMVs— it is short by 1,400, according to its formal equipping table, but can repair a number of those damaged and recovered, if it can acquire the spare parts. The unit also lacks machine guns (.50 caliber, M240s, M249s) and the spare parts to repair damaged ones. The Iraq Train and Equip Fund (ITEF) package includes HMMVs, but they are not yet available because of limited production capacity. The United States expects delivery of 115 HMMVs later this summer. Machine guns are available in Kuwait, but as with the HMMVs, the United States and Iraq will have to decide whether to prioritize delivery to CTS or ISF brigades.

- A final point on CTS: In order to rebuild the force, the U.S. and coalition SOF advisers have revised the training program to add more classes of shorter duration. By next January, according to the plan, the ranks of the three Iraqi special operations brigades should be back to 11,000 on duty and 2,000 in the selection and training pipeline. This assumes a continuing level of attrition. The newer force will be trained as light infantry and will be less experienced. While the CTS does have a few forward observers, and is training more, the new ones will obviously be less experienced.

- Third, the Kurdish security forces (KSF) include the pesh merga and the interior ministry Zerevani. They are capable forces that have pushed back ISIL, in the process expanding territory held by the Kurdistan Regional Government by 30 percent, and they are an important part of the effort. However, they have, I would argue, largely achieved their objectives of defending predominantly Kurdish areas and moved into defensive mode. ISIL will certainly continue to test their defensive line, which stretches 1,200 kilometers. But the KSF are likely to play only a supporting role in any offensive to liberate Mosul, and they have not yet committed explicitly to a number of specific requests for supporting roles in that operation. Moreover, they are not likely to deploy to Anbar or other purely Arab areas. The point of this analysis is not to diminish the valor and commitment of the most capable ally the United States has in this fight, but rather to note that the Kurds are not the silver bullet that some would wish them to be.

- The KSF has received at least 50 million rounds of ammunition, thousands of small arms, and more than 8,500 anti-tank weapons donated by coalition countries directly to the KSF. The Kurds seek heavy weaponry, and the United States will have to decide how to address the many requests. Some U.S. officials think that the Kurds are relatively well supplied at this time, especially compared with other elements seeking support.

- U.S. forces are supporting the KSF through a combined operations center and advisory support at multiple echelons. This includes advisory support to the brigade level.

- Fourth, the program to raise Sunni tribal forces to fight ISIL is still nascent. This is a complicated picture: 11,000 have been officially "enrolled" by the Iraqi government. However, only 2,300 have been trained, equipped, and advised by U.S. forces, and not all have passed the two U.S. vetting processes.[6] Even if all 11,000 were armed tomorrow, they do not represent a silver bullet. They will not be heavily armed, equipped with armored vehicles, or trained for combined arms maneuver. They will primarily serve as local defense forces, though they can have greater effect if coordinated with other forces. The arming of Sunnis will be tremendously important as a political signal of inclusivity. The Mosul Fighting Forces (MFF) are another group recruited from former policemen. Some of those I talked to in the north said that both the MFF and Sunni recruits are barely hanging on, without salaries, arms, ammunition, or other support from either the Iraqi or the Kurdish governments.

  - The only place where the desired synergy between ISF and Sunni tribes has been achieved to date is in western Anbar, where the Iraqi 7th Army, the al-Jazeera and al-Badia Command (JBOC) command, and elements of four tribes mentored by coalition SOF are all working together.

---

[6] One vetting process ascertains that no member is credibly alleged to have committed human rights abuses as required by the Leahy Amendment, and the other ascertains that the inductee has no ties to Iran or to al Qaeda or its successors in Iraq.

- Fifth, the Iraqi Shia armed groups are by all accounts motivated, organized, capable, and equipped. They number some 80,000–100,000.[7] They are composed of three elements: 1) the volunteers who responded to Ayatollah Sistani's call to defend the country, 2) a collection of newer Shia militias, and 3) the long-standing Shia groups—the Badr Organization, the Sadrist Promised Day Brigade, the Kataib Hezbollah, and the Asaib Ahl Al-Haq.[8]

  - After leading Shia cleric Grand Ayatollah Ali Al-Sistani issued a call for Iraqis to defend their country last summer, many of these militias were reinvigorated, and Shia volunteers in particular responded to Sistani's call. The Iraqi government formed a Popular Mobilization Committee to organize these Popular Mobilization Forces. This has been the nominal vehicle for corralling the disparate paramilitary forces, both Shia and Sunni. Prime Minister Abadi is formally the commander in chief of the Popular Mobilization Forces, and the chain of command goes from him to his national security adviser, to Mohandis, and then to whatever field chain they designate. The current request by the United States is that that chain report to the ISF chain of command if those forces wish to receive air support in ISF-led operations.

  - The Badr, Kataib Hezbollah, and Asaib Ahl Al-Haq have been in the forefront of Popular Mobilization Forces activity in Diyala, Salahuddin, the Baghdad belts, and now in Anbar. Furthermore, Kataib Hezbollah commander Abu Mahdi Al-Mohandis is the deputy chief of the government's overall coordinating body, the Popular Mobilization Committee. He and Badr leader and member of Parliament Hadi Al-Amiri recently visited the Baghdad command center. They and Asaib Ahl Al-Haq leader Qais Khazali regularly appear on the battlefield. CTS commander Gen. Kenani told me that there is a representative from the Popular Mobilization Committee in the Combined Joint Operations Center.

---

[7] For one source using the 100,000-troop estimate, see Kenneth Katzman, "Iraq: Politics, Security, and U.S. Policy," Congressional Research Service Report for Congress, May 26, 2015, available at: https://www.fas.org/sgp/crs/mideast/RS21968.pdf.

[8] The Badr and Sadr elements are established political parties with paramilitary forces. The Badr Corps formed in the 1980s with Iranian support to fight Saddam Hussein in the Iran-Iraq war. In 2011, Badr split from the Islamic Supreme Revolutionary Council of Iraq in order to become a separate politico-military organization. Members of the Badr Corps, as it was also known, were included in the first Iraqi units formed after the U.S. invasion, the Iraqi Civil Defense Corps, which later became the Iraqi Army. During the U.S. invasion in 2003, Moqtada al-Sadr founded another politico-military organization whose militias were largely demobilized after 2010 or converted into social service organizations until the upsurge of ISIL violence in 2014. Badr is part of the dominant State of Law coalition, while the Sadrists won 32 seats in the April 2014 elections. Kataib Hizbollah was trained by Iran's Quds Force, as was Asaib Ahl al-Haq, a splinter group of the Sadr's original militia, the Mahdi Army. Both of these groups were implicated in attacks on American troops. A short history of these groups can be found in Katzman, 2015.

– One of the most surprising things I heard on this trip from a number of U.S. and coalition officers was the view that the United States must bow to reality and be more proactive in coordinating with these forces on the battlefield. Doing so, they argued, will produce more gains in the anti-ISIL fight. A more active U.S. role vis a vis the Shia militias could also entail efforts to mitigate the two widely acknowledged risks of their currently large and growing role. The first risk is that these forces may well commit atrocities or sectarian cleansing, as occurred in Diyala province, and thus spur even more recruits to ISIL.[9] The second risk is that the militias' battlefield successes will further strengthen their political and military clout, which could well lead eventually to the Lebanonization of Iraq (i.e., the long-term entrenchment of militia power). The two larger groups, Badr and perhaps the Sadrists, are already established political forces, and they might be prepared to see the long-term benefits of an effort to bring their militias firmly under government control and eventually integrate them into ISF or National Guard structures.

- Sixth, to briefly sketch the status of forces in Syria, ISIL and the Al Nusra Front (ANF), which is an Al-Qaeda affiliate, hold the most territory. At this time, Assad's removal would likely favor those two forces. However, the Syrian Kurdish Yekineyen Parastina Gel (YPG) or People's Protection Units and Free Syria Army recently allied in a collaboration called Burkan al-Furat (Euphrates Volcano). They are making significant gains on the Turkish border, notably the capture of Tel Abyad, and with it the closure of ISIL's main external line of communication. The Turkish government has been opposed to supporting the YPG.

  – The U.S. train and equip effort to build the New Syria Force (NSF) is extremely nascent, with no forces fielded and fewer than 200 currently in training. The original plan was to raise a force of 15,000 over three years, but one officer who worked on this program from its inception characterized the effort as "absolutely too little, too late." Another officer characterized the value of the NSF in more political terms, as a force that could serve as a boots-on-the-ground supporter of a post-Assad regime reached through a negotiated departure of Assad. However, the military facts on the ground suggest that ISIL and ANF, the latter of which has increasingly attracted support of more moderate opposition fighters

---

[9] Human Rights Watch documented Shia militias' abuses in Amerli, Diyala, after anti-ISIL operations there in 2014. See "After Liberation Came Destruction: Iraqi Militias and the Aftermath of Amerli," Human Rights Watch, March 18, 2015.

like the Islamic Front and even secular groups, may play a more significant role in determining Syria's future. Syria's prolonged fragmentation or an outright victory by radical Islamists would appear to be the two most likely scenarios at this point.

Assessment of U.S. Military Effort

The lack of capability and capacity of the ISF means that any ground effort will have to depend on the totality of forces available in the short term. Therefore, effective coordination and advisory support to those elements at the operational level is the most urgent need. Coordinating with Shia militias is controversial, but it should be noted that previous U.S. military commands (the Multinational Forces-Iraq and the International Security Assistance Force in Afghanistan) both created engagement cells that talked to adversaries. Engagement may provide avenues to mitigate the negative effects. Finally, additional measures may improve the efficacy of the air campaign, though ground forces and not air will be decisive in this largely urban hybrid campaign. The following section offers observations and recommendations regarding the three main elements of the U.S. military line of effort.

- *Advise and assist.* The Iraqi effort is critically lacking coordinated planning and execution of operations. This caused the fall of Ramadi. This month, the administration announced a decision to send 450 U.S. military personnel to the Taqqadum base in Anbar. Sending advisers to the area commands has been under discussion for months, as the Chairman of the Joint Chiefs of Staff indicated in his testimony last week. It was the right step but belated, and it should be expanded to other area commands.

  - The most critical need is for advisory assistance at the area commands to coordinate operations among all the stovepiped organizations (army, CTS, police, and militias) to coordinate and improve combined arms operations, support, and sustainment; increase visibility of all forces; and exercise restraint on abuses. The critical area commands are Anbar, Salah al-Din, and Ninewa. The Baghdad Operations Command is operating much as these commands should, with a capable commander who is also actively recruiting to fill his force. Placing Joint Terminal Air Controllers (JTACs) at these area commands and at trusted brigade commands' forward command posts can help coordinate fires and speed accurate targeting. In addition, U.S. SOF have identified an available satellite radio in Kuwait in U.S. army stocks. These satellite radios and Thurayas can provide a speedier and more-accurate targeting solution without putting combat advisers into tactical units.

— Somewhat to my surprise, most officers did **not** argue for tactical combat advisers or JTACs below the brigade level. The commanders do want the discretion to move advisers as the brigade commander moves. Moving advisers to the battalion level and below dramatically increases the footprint required to support them (including air support, medevac, quick reaction forces, and logistic support), as well as the risk to U.S. forces. It also increases the dependency of the forces, a lesson that U.S. SOF and others have learned in recent years.

— Finally, the Combined Joint Operations Center was seen by several officers as too narrowly focused as a strike cell. Given the lack of coordination among the varied armed forces, the center could be usefully transformed into a general headquarters that plans and coordinates all the stovepiped organizations on the battlefield.

- *Train and equip (T&E).* A long-term commitment to building a professional security force is needed for Iraq to avoid the prospect of Lebanonization. The current T&E program's scale is limited and should be expanded: The eight brigades represent only a fraction of the force. This will take time as units are deployed in operations, and recruitment is constrained by Iraq's budget deficit. The scope is also limited: Institutional changes need to be an equal focus of the current effort to correct the structural problems, including recruiting with nonsectarian standards, consolidating units, ending the ghost soldiers, and instituting leadership standards and accountability systems. (The Iraqi army did not train since 2010, and what the United States did help build was destroyed in the interim.)

    — The U.S. security assistance process operates on a two-year cycle that is not sufficiently agile for wartime needs. Also, it does not supply training ammunition and other training needs. A tailored security force assistance package is needed. Finally, commanders say they need small amounts of flexible funds for emergent needs.

- *Air campaign.* The air campaign is being conducted according to three basic principles: avoid civilian casualties; obtain Iraqi approval; and do not put U.S. combat forces in frontline positions, which would significantly increase the risk of U.S. casualties. A more aggressive air campaign that involved greater numbers of civilian casualties would risk increasing the alienation of the largely Sunni population in these areas and a wider backlash from public opinion. However, a review of the process appears warranted to determine whether greater effects may be achieved. By some accounts, Iraqi units in contact may wait up to an hour for air support, but I have not verified those statements.

- Several steps might be considered to increase the effects of the air campaign under the current procedures and rules of engagement. One obvious step is to increase the amount of intelligence, surveillance, and reconnaissance assets and analysts dedicated to Iraq and Syria and to increase the deliberate targeting. Another step, as stated above, is to accelerate the targeting cycle by supplying radios to Iraqi units that accurately mark friendly locations and permit more reliable and secure communications. More indigenous forces can be trained to assist in target development. Placing advisers at area commands should also have a significant effect on the speed of the targeting process. The authority to order strikes when the proper assessments have been conducted could be distributed more widely. The effects of these steps could be assessed before considering further revisions to policy and procedure.

The Overall Conduct of the Strategy and Lines of Effort

The U.S. effort has suffered from some confusion about who is in charge of synchronizing the multiple lines of effort in the strategy. (There is even confusion about the number of lines of effort: Just in the past month, officials have stated that there are nine, five, and six lines). In particular, the political and military efforts are not closely synchronized. A logical division of labor would be for the U.S. embassy to focus on political and institutional issues while the military focuses on the operational and tactical issues.

A major surge in the political line of effort is warranted. This should focus not just on Prime Minister Abadi but on the major political blocs represented in parliament. Under the majoritarian system in which the Shia majority has the winning votes, the priority should be to engage with the Shia parties and leaders, and secondarily to encourage the three separate Sunni blocs to come together on a vision for the proposed National Guard and over the longer term on a federalized system with greater decentralization.

In the near term, passage of legislation on the National Guard could be a huge boost for the counter-ISIL campaign—but only if it is a version that wins Sunni support. Coalition diplomats might be helpful in exploring whether there is a compromise on the National Guard legislation that would allow the Guard commander to be nominated by the Provincial Governor and/or jointly appointed, rather than solely by Baghdad. It would be hard to overestimate the positive effect of legislation that gives Sunnis some control over securing their areas, as well as a possible path for incorporation of militia members into regular entities of the government.

The U.S. government cannot impose its will, and its voice is not necessarily the most influential one in Baghdad at this point. It may be that the diplomatic community in Baghdad can form a contact group to support the search for political compromises. The cleavages are deep and may not be bridged, or at least for some time. By the same token, the United States will have to accept what the Iraqi government determines to be its operational priorities in terms of Baghdad, Anbar, Bayji, and Mosul. Shaping operations for Mosul can accelerate as the ISF capacity increases.

An urgent priority should be facilitating the return of residents to Tikrit and helping rebuild their city under their elected officials' governance. Otherwise, Tikrit threatens to become a very negative symbol for Sunnis. I met with several displaced residents, who told me that only in recent days, 1,000 families have been allowed back. Even 300 tribesmen from Al Alam who fought for the liberation of Tikrit have not been welcomed back. Hospitals, homes, and businesses were looted and destroyed, and services remain scarce. Between the new focus on Ramadi and the ongoing preoccupation with Mosul, Tikrit threatens to be lost in the shuffle.

The United States has a difficult time, it is often noted, gaining traction in the counter-ISIL information and messaging space. While this is primarily a job for the Iraqis and the wider Muslim community, the incoming two-star commander of our Combined Forces Land Component Command in Baghdad and the current brigade commander are rightly focused on ways to counter ISIL's media operations and promote effective communications policies by the area commands. It would seem that the most powerful counter-ISIL messages are those delivered by disaffected former fighters.

Finally, regarding the other lines of effort, the Gulf countries' relatively weak roles are noteworthy, although finally Saudi Arabia has opened its embassy in Baghdad. Given the Gulf states' concerns about Iraq's close ties with Iran, Iraqi overtures to Gulf states may be beneficial. The other glaring fact is the continued lax visa and border policies of Turkey. Turkey's priority has been to seek the ouster of Syrian president Bashar Assad rather than shut off the flow of foreign fighters, but the recent elections and pending change in government in Turkey may provide an opportunity to secure further measures to stem the flow of fighters and resources.

Assessment of Options

To answer the overall question of this hearing—are we on the right path?—ISIL's continuing strength indicates that adjustments in the current approach are necessary. The timeline is also likely to be more extended than previously estimated. There are three theoretical options: 1) improve the current strategy of working through partners, 2) launch more-aggressive unilateral measures, or 3) fall back to a containment strategy.

The best strategy is to defeat and destroy ISIL through a partnered approach, because if the Iraqis and Syrians can fight and win this war, they will own that victory. This is an excruciatingly difficult case, however, and it involves dealing with less-than-ideal partners, as outlined here. The strategy may be failing not because it cannot work, but because it is not being adequately resourced. In particular, the advisory effort has not been robustly resourced and implemented at the operational level. Four specific steps are recommended in the short term. First, the United States should send advisers to the area commands and the CTS brigade level to assist in coordination, planning, and execution of operations. Second, the Combined Joint Operations Center should also expand its focus on planning and coordination of forces at the national level, supported with adequate intelligence collection and analysis. Third, delivery of the needed vehicles, weapons, and spare parts should be accelerated. Fourth, the provision of satellite radios, which are available but not part of the programmed delivery, should be approved and prioritized for delivery to the Iraqi special operations units and other trusted units. To have maximum effect, this suite of measures should be implemented in conjunction immediately. Finally, in order to have lasting effect, these short-term measures should be coupled with a long-term commitment to building a professional Iraqi security force, competing with Iranian influence, and trying to help Iraqis forge political compromises that may be several years in the making.

The second option of adopting more unilateral measures is not viable unless the United States is prepared to enter into conflict with the government of Iraq. The government of Iraq is not likely to accept a U.S. combat role or other unilateral actions, and such options also include significantly increased risk to U.S. forces. For example, directly arming Kurds and Sunnis would not be welcomed by the central government. Unilateral bombing without Iraqi participation in the decision-making would also not likely be welcome. Putting JTACs with Iraqi battalions or even lower echelons amounts to inserting them into combat and would require deploying many more troops in addition to those advisers. This much larger footprint would include quick reaction forces, medical evacuation airlift, and close air support, along with the support personnel each of those elements requires. Another idea, isolated insertions of combat forces to retake key areas, would hazard a longer-term combat commitment if ISIL proved a significant match for U.S. troops.

Taking these steps unilaterally would likely create another source of opposition—including potential armed opposition from Iraq, Shia militias, or Iran.

The third alternative available is containment, which might include a combination of continued attrition from the air and perhaps by SOF, coupled with greater support to neighboring countries like Jordan to add a containment dimension. Should the partnered approach fail, the United States may have to fall back to this option. We should recognize that this approach would amount largely to "mowing the grass," and, given porous borders and a fluid enemy that already has global reach, containment in practice may prove no more effective. However, this option should be studied and some elements of containment are probably warranted at this stage, particularly to insulate Jordan and Lebanon from the destabilizing political and economic effects of the massive refugee populations.

In summary, the United States faces a most difficult challenge in partnering with the government of Iraq. The U.S. and Iraqi governments are aligned in the desire to counter ISIL; however, the Iraqi government and the Shia majority at large have not yet come to a consensus about incorporation of Sunnis into the political and military institutions of the country. Sunni exclusion, from the U.S. perspective, is a major driver of the ISIL engine, yet Iraq's Shiites remain prisoners of their past. They may eventually reach a federal solution that pacifies Iraq, though it is also possible that the country will dissolve. How Iraq arrives at decentralization or dissolution will matter greatly, as new conflicts of extended duration can open up in that process.

In the meantime, the United States may be guaranteeing the failure of the Abadi government, a well-intentioned if weak partner, by its relatively slow, fitful, and ambivalent support, particularly compared with the support offered by Iran. Some U.S. observers believe Iraq is already irrevocably in the Iranian orbit, but U.S. actions may make that a self-fulfilling prophecy. Highly conditioned support at this stage may serve primarily to weaken Abadi in the face of less palatable options. There is no guarantee that his government will survive or succeed, but it would be a shame if he failed for want of U.S. support in the face of the extremely resilient ISIL threat.

Linda Robinson
Senior International Policy Analyst
RAND Corporation

Education
B.A. in political science, Swarthmore College

Linda Robinson is a senior international policy analyst at the RAND Corporation. Her areas of expertise include national security strategy, international affairs, U.S. foreign policy, security force assistance, special operations forces, irregular warfare and stability operations. She has worked in South Asia, Iraq, the Middle East, and Latin America as a journalist and researcher. Her current research centers on ISIL, political warfare. political transitions, building partner capacity, and special operations forces. Robinson has authored joint concepts, designed workshops and tabletop exercises on complex contingency operations, and provided political-military and strategy analysis to various commands. She was author of a Council on Foreign Relations special report on the future of special operations forces (2013). Her most recent book, One Hundred Victories: Special Ops and the Future of American Warfare, was published in paperback in 2013. She is also the author of a book on Iraq, Tell Me How This Ends (2008), as well as Masters of Chaos (2004) and Intervention or Neglect (1991). She is on the board of the National Defense University, chair of the Army War College board, and a senior fellow at Joint Special Operations University.

DISCLOSURE FORM FOR WITNESSES
COMMITTEE ON ARMED SERVICES
U.S. HOUSE OF REPRESENTATIVES

INSTRUCTION TO WITNESSES: Rule 11, clause 2(g)(5), of the Rules of the U.S. House of Representatives for the 114th Congress requires nongovernmental witnesses appearing before House committees to include in their written statements a curriculum vitae and a disclosure of the amount and source of any federal contracts or grants (including subcontracts and subgrants), or contracts or payments originating with a foreign government, received during the current and two previous calendar years either by the witness or by an entity represented by the witness and related to the subject matter of the hearing. This form is intended to assist witnesses appearing before the House Committee on Armed Services in complying with the House rule. Please note that a copy of these statements, with appropriate redactions to protect the witness's personal privacy (including home address and phone number) will be made publicly available in electronic form not later than one day after the witness's appearance before the committee. Witnesses may list additional grants, contracts, or payments on additional sheets, if necessary.

Witness name: Linda Robinson

Capacity in which appearing: (check one)

◯ Individual

◉ Representative

If appearing in a representative capacity, name of the company, association or other entity being represented: RAND Corporation

Federal Contract or Grant Information: If you or the entity you represent before the Committee on Armed Services has contracts (including subcontracts) or grants (including subgrants) with the federal government, please provide the following information:

2015

Federal grant/ contract	Federal agency	Dollar value	Subject of contract or grant
Contract	Office of the Secretary of Defense	$19,597,772	NDRI
Contract	U.S. Army	$21,166,940	Arroyo Center
Contract	U.S. Air Force	$27,236,632	Project Air Force

2014

Federal grant/ contract	Federal agency	Dollar value	Subject of contract or grant
Contract	Office of the Secretary of Defense	63,759,734	NDRI
Contract	U.S. Army	39,378,840	Arroyo Center
Contract	U.S. Air Force	46,055,802	Project Air Force

2013

Federal grant/ contract	Federal agency	Dollar value	Subject of contract or grant
Contract	Office of the Secretary of Defense	63,539,233	NDRI
Contract	U.S. Army	35,033,902	Arroyo Center
Contract	U.S. Air Force	34,399,281	Project Air Force

Foreign Government Contract or Payment Information: If you or the entity you represent before the Committee on Armed Services has contracts or payments originating from a foreign government, please provide the following information:

2015

Foreign contract/ payment	Foreign government	Dollar value	Subject of contract or payment
Please see attached supplement			

2014

Foreign contract/ payment	Foreign government	Dollar value	Subject of contract or payment
Please see attached supplement			

2013

Foreign contract/ payment	Foreign government	Dollar value	Subject of contract or payment
Please see attached supplement			

Aligning Means and Ends, Policies and Strategy in the War on ISIL

Michael Eisenstadt

**Testimony submitted to the House Armed Services Subcommittee on
Emerging Threats and Capabilities
June 24, 2015**

Chairman Wilson, ranking member Langevin, distinguished members of the subcommittee: thank you for giving me this opportunity to appear before you today to discuss this matter of great importance to our nation.

Recent gains by Islamic State in Iraq and the Levant (ISIL) in Iraq and Syria mark major setbacks in the nearly year-old campaign against the group. These developments undermine Obama administration claims of progress in the war, and highlight fundamental flaws in the administration's strategy that need to be rectified if the United States and its coalition of 60-plus states are to succeed. President Obama was only partially right when he said several weeks ago that America lacks a "complete strategy" for dealing with ISIL because of Iraq's lack of commitment. In fact, much of the dysfunction in U.S. strategy derives from American policies, the policies of partners in the counter-ISIL campaign, and the policies of the Iraqi government.

For starters, the United States needs to address the means-ends mismatch in its strategy. It has devoted inadequate resources in pursuit of a goal — to "degrade and eventually destroy" ISIL — whose ultimate objective is likely to remain unattainable for the foreseeable future. This is due to ISIL's resilience, the weakness of America's regional partners, and the incoherence of current U.S. strategy.

Resilient Organization. ISIL's predecessor, al-Qaeda in Iraq (AQI), was defeated between 2007-2011 before returning in its current guise. Its ability to rebound from this blow is rooted in a number of factors.

For its supporters, ISIL's ideology embodies "true" Islam, unsullied by the demands of political competition or undue concern for the opinion of unbelievers. They are likewise unbothered by the criticism of establishment Muslim clerics, whom they regard as servants of an illegitimate state system. For this reason, it is difficult to delegitimize ISIL on religious grounds. Administration efforts to use critical statements by mainstream clerics to do so are likely to only succeed on the margins.

ISIL had previously survived as an underground terrorist network and could do so again if it were run to ground, drawing on skills honed during its years in the shadows. It can, moreover, draw on financial and manpower reserves from around the world (though the coalition is trying to stem the flow of both), and it has recently started taking on the attributes of a decentralized network, with jihadist groups around the region pledging fealty (*bay'ah*) to it. This will likely ensure the survival of the ISIL brand in some shape or form, even if its flagship operation in Iraq and Syria is defeated.

The operational environment in the Middle East is likewise conducive to ISIL's continued survival. Since the popular uprisings of 2011, the region has been increasingly characterized by weak and failing states which lack the capacity to root out terrorist networks or defeat insurgent groups, and the emergence of ungoverned spaces which serve as safe havens for such organizations (such as eastern Syria). The zero-sum politics that prevails in the region helped bring about this state of affairs, and will ensure the survival of groups like ISIL, which feed on the grievances and aspirations of the region's Sunni population.

While ISIL enjoys a number of strengths in the realm of military leadership, organization, and tactical virtuosity, it is also bedeviled by numerous vulnerabilities: overextended forces; a propensity to alienate its support base; internal divisions between Iraqis, Arabs, and non-Arabs; uncertain finance streams; and its landlocked position — though it has proven particularly adept at exploiting its porous border with Turkey. Yet, the weakness of the Arab state system has prevented America's regional partners from capitalizing on these vulnerabilities.

Thus, while the United States and its partners can potentially degrade ISIL, they will not be able to destroy it — at least anytime soon. In the long run, without addressing those factors that contribute to the appeal of groups like ISIL and al-Qaeda, the best the United States can hope for is to destroy its overt military formations, to dismantle the administrative machinery of its state, and to push it underground — at least in Iraq. But as recent events have shown, efforts to date have borne only mixed results. While U.S. military operations may be attriting ISIL forces, and its partners have retaken ground previously lost to the group, the coalition has not degraded the overall capabilities of an organization that has demonstrated impressive regenerative powers, and which remains on the offensive on a number of important fronts.

Yet, the solution is not another major U.S. ground commitment to the region. The American people would not support such a deployment, and even if they did — and the United States were to put 50,000 service-members on the ground, were to defeat ISIL's military forces, and were to dismantle its state — without a change in the nature of politics in Iraq (and other troubled states in the region), U.S. forces would almost certainly have to return again 3-5 years hence to deal with this problem. The Middle East has an insatiable appetite for American blood and treasure that the Washington should not indulge; it would do better to avoid this vicious cycle.

Walking away is not an option either. The Obama administration's experience of the past six years shows that "if you don't visit the Middle East, it will visit you." The challenge is to find the right balance; the United States and its coalition partners need to adjust their light footprint strategy to ensure that the coalition can gradually roll back ISIL while avoiding additional major setbacks and addressing the factors that contribute to its appeal.

Disjointed Strategy. The United States and its partners have often pursued policies that have strengthened salafi-jihadist groups such as ISIL, thereby undermining the U.S.-led campaign. Doubling down on the current approach in Iraq and Syria — as promised three weeks ago in Paris by U.S. Deputy Secretary of State Tony Blinken — without altering policies that work at cross-purposes to the coalition military effort will only serve to further complicate matters.

First, Washington needs to acknowledge that its own policies contributed to the rise of groups like Jabhat al-Nusra and ISIL in Syria, and the return of ISIL to Iraq. American inaction in the face of the Syrian civil war and the Maliki government's exclusionary politics in Iraq, the widespread perception in the region that the United States is tacitly aligned with Iran, and the fact that America's first military strikes in Iraq were to save Yezidis, Turkmen, and Kurds — anybody but Sunni Arabs — were a recruiting boon for jihadists.

Second, America's Syria policy has been hostage to its Iran policy. The administration has not done more to militarily assist the Syria opposition at least in part to avoid jeopardizing a nuclear deal with Iran. Yet the prospect of a deal has not constrained the Islamic Republic in Syria. The United States must pursue its own interests in Syria, which means increasing support for what remains of the "moderate" opposition there, even while pursuing a nuclear deal with Iran. Otherwise, fighters will continue to flock to extremist groups to fight the Assad regime and their Iranian allies.

Third, the United States insists that it is training and equipping the "moderate" Syrian opposition to fight ISIL, while the opposition, as well as America's partners in this effort — Turkey, Jordan, Saudi Arabia, and Qatar — insist that it fight the Assad regime. The U.S. stance is likely to stymie efforts to recruit Syrian opposition fighters who are not interested in fighting ISIL, while the divergence between Washington and its partners on this matter is a formula for disaster.

Fourth, the success of America's counter-ISIL strategy is hostage to the politics and policies of its regional partners. Several have provided or permitted their citizens to provide financial and military support to jihadist groups, and some still do. Some of this aid has found its way to ISIL, while members of these groups have sometimes pledged fealty en masse to ISIL. Foreign support for jihadists often redounds to the benefit of ISIL, because it is perceived by many to be the most successful jihadist brand. Meanwhile, Iraqi Prime Minister Haydar al-Abadi has not done much to change the zero-sum politics in Iraq that created the conditions for the return of AQI in the guise of ISIL; efforts at Sunni outreach by Baghdad remain stillborn.

Finally, the United States will not succeed in its fight against ISIL in Iraq if it does not succeed in its fight against ISIL in Syria. Eastern Syria served in the past as a safe haven for ISIL and continues to serve as a support base for its operations in Iraq. If ISIL is not expelled from eastern Syria, it will continue to destabilize Iraq from there. For this reason, America needs to replace its Iraq-first strategy with one that pursues a simultaneous two-front fight against ISIL in Iraq and Syria. This will convince Syrians that Washington is concerned about their fate, and improve prospects for the train and equip program for the moderate Syrian opposition that could divert personnel and materiel now going to more extreme groups.

It is not too late to correct course. The fires now consuming Iraq and Syria will, tragically, continue to burn for years to come, and the outcome of these struggles is far from assured. The United States can make a difference if it remains politically and militarily engaged, creating opportunities, while exploiting those that arise.

Aligning Means and Ends, Policy and Strategy. So what would a prudent and effective course-adjustment involve? In Iraq, this would mean more reconnaissance drones (most now support operations in Afghanistan), more joint terminal attack controllers and special forces — with rules of engagement that enable them to accompany Iraqi units into combat, more airpower, and more personnel devoted to the train and equip effort for the Iraqi Security Forces and Kurdish peshmerga. It would also entail more pressure on the Iraqi government to permit the arming and training of Sunni Arab tribesmen as militiamen — to gain Sunni buy-in and create a force to fight ISIL in predominantly Sunni regions of Iraq.

The United States likewise needs to rethink its approach to train and equip. It needs to work with the Iraqi government to find solutions to persistent problems with military leadership, unit cohesion, and motivation. It needs to constantly emphasize to Baghdad that if it fails to get the politics of the counter-ISIL campaign right — if the security forces continue to be perceived as driven by sectarian or political considerations — and if corruption remains rampant, the prospects for the counter-ISIL campaign will be dismal. The United States should look to successful Middle Eastern insurgent groups, militias, and armies for leadership and team-building models that have worked well within the region's cultural context.

Finally, the coalition needs to avoid additional reverses as occurred in Ramadi. The perception that momentum has shifted against ISIL is key to success in Iraq (and Syria). New victories for ISIL — even if ephemeral — will be fatal to efforts to rebuild American credibility and to convince Sunni Arabs sitting on the fence to join the coalition against ISIL.

In Syria, the United States should likewise beef up its effort to train and equip "moderate" opposition groups, while dropping its prior insistence that these groups fight only ISIL. These groups have been decimated in the past 1-2 years (due in part to a lack of American support), and while this most recent effort has gotten off to a slow start, money and weapons have a way of generating their own demand.

The United States should not, for now, fixate on numbers. Quality is more important than quantity, as the Syrian battlespace is highly fragmented, and the challenge is to create organizations that can seize and hold ground, hold their own in local fights, and effectively govern small, defensible enclaves. Perhaps the most important task is to demonstrate that the United States is finally serious about supporting the opposition, in order to attract new recruits and win back defectors who opportunistically migrated from the Free Syrian Army to better resourced (and frequently more extreme) groups. And by more strongly supporting the moderate opposition, the U.S. will be able to more effectively pressure allies to pare back support for jihadist opposition groups.

To deal with the Assad regime barrel-bomb threat, the United States should work to create a serious anti-aircraft artillery capability in the opposition groups it supports, while avoiding the provision of MANPADs in large numbers due to proliferation fears. Though low-tech, flak is highly lethal; even when it does not succeed in shooting down aircraft, it forces enemy pilots to deliver their unguided ordnance from higher altitudes, thereby degrading their accuracy. And it is useful in ground combat.

In addition to receiving military training, U.S.-supported opposition groups should be trained in governance and administration, to enable them to create secure enclaves for local residents and internally displaced persons. Making this the principal criteria by which opposition groups are assessed may be one way for the United States and its partners to reconcile their divergent views regarding the role of the opposition vis-à-vis the Assad regime and ISIL — at least for now — and address Washington's concerns that Tehran would use the ramp-up of the train and equip effort as a pretext to encourage pro-Iranian militias to attack U.S. forces in Iraq.

In sum, closing the gap between means and ends in the counter-ISIL strategy is a necessary, but not sufficient condition for success. If the United States is to succeed in Iraq and Syria, it will also need to alter its policies — and those of its partners — which have greatly complicated the military effort, and more closely align its policies with the counter-ISIL strategy. Should it prove unwilling or unable to do so, the prospects for success against ISIL will become close to nil. The success of the U.S. strategy, then, depends in part on its allies' politics and policy choices—and this is its Achilles' heel.

The Defeat Mechanism. If ISIL's military is to be defeated and its "Islamic state" dismantled, the United States will need to exploit its vulnerabilities and sharpen the contradictions inherent in ISIL rule. This will require intensified action along military, economic, and psychological lines of effort to create synergies capable of producing decisive results:

Military operations should attrite ISIL's combat power, hit symbolic and substantive targets associated with its rule (e.g., key leaders), and pressure ISIL simultaneously in Iraq and Syria — prioritizing neither, while employing different means in each—in order to overextend ISIL and render it vulnerable to internal uprisings and external attack.

The United States should likewise continue to disrupt ISIL's oil production and smuggling activities to choke off its revenue stream and resources available for public services, governance, and economic activities. This will hopefully stir discontent and unrest in areas it controls. Disrupting the criminal activities that have traditionally been its main source of income will, however, be much harder.

The United States should likewise strive to transform the psychological environment in Iraq and Syria by creating the perception, mainly through military means, that ISIL's days are numbered. Such an effort may induce less committed supporters or members to defect or turn on the group; deter prospective foreign fighters from joining it; and embolden subject populations to rise up against its overstretched forces.

However, military reverses, as recently occurred in Ramadi, undermine such efforts. They deter Sunnis from undertaking the kinds of uprisings that will be essential to defeat ISIL by instilling fears that after rising up, they might once again find themselves under ISIL rule and subject to retribution.

Efforts to transform the psychological environment should likewise include attempts to convince Syrians that the "moderate" opposition constitutes a viable third way between the regime and ISIL, and to convince Iraqi Sunnis that the government of Prime Minister Abadi offers a better future than does ISIL. Offers by the Iraqi government of administrative and security federalism to the largely Sunni provinces of Iraq will be crucial here.

Undermining ISIL's Appeal. The main purpose of ISIL's prodigious and sophisticated media efforts is to enhance its appeal, burnish its ideological credentials, and build up its brand. Because so much of ISIL's appeal derives from its aura of military invincibility, its defeat would show that ISIL was just another failed ideological movement that brought only ruin to those who embrace it. Moreover, its defeat would mean no caliphate, no Islamic utopia, no glory and adventure, no opportunity to dominate others, no spoils of war, and no sex slaves — the things that have drawn so many to embrace its cause. Through military victories, the United States can defeat ISIL's media effort by demonstrating that the tide is turning against it and that its days are numbered. The defeat of ISIL is thus key to undermining its appeal, discrediting its ideology, and demolishing its brand. And this, ultimately, is the most important goal of the counter-ISIL military campaign. But the administration's current light footprint approach permits ISIL to continue to accrue victories that undercut this effort.

Finally, the U.S. needs to figure out how al-Qaeda and its affiliates as well as Iran fit into all of this. For if the coalition enfeebles or defeats ISIL only to clear the way for primacy of Jabhat al-Nusra in Syria and the expansion of Iranian influence in Mesopotamia and the Levant, the United States will have only succeeded in adding fuel to the region's raging sectarian and geopolitical conflicts. The sooner Washington realizes this, the sooner it can work to avert an even greater disaster down the road that it may be inadvertently abetting.

Michael Eisenstadt is Kahn Fellow, and Director of the Military and Security Studies Program at The Washington Institute for Near East Policy. He can be reached at meisenstadt@washingtoninstitute.org.

Mr. Michael Eisenstadt
Kahn Fellow and Director, Military & Security Studies Program
The Washington Institute

Michael Eisenstadt is the Kahn Fellow and director of The Washington Institute's Military and Security Studies Program. A specialist in Persian Gulf and Arab-Israeli security affairs, he has published widely on irregular and conventional warfare, and nuclear weapons proliferation in the Middle East.

Prior to joining the Institute in 1989, Mr. Eisenstadt worked as a military analyst with the U.S. government.

Mr. Eisenstadt served for twenty-six years as an officer in the U.S. Army Reserve before retiring in 2010. His military service included active-duty stints in Iraq with the United States Forces-Iraq headquarters (2010) and the Human Terrain System Assessment Team (2008); in Jerusalem, the West Bank, and Jordan with the U.S. Security Coordinator (USSC) for Israel and the Palestinian Authority (2008-2009); at U.S. Central Command headquarters and on the Joint Staff during Operation Enduring Freedom and the planning for Operation Iraqi Freedom (2001-2002); and in Turkey and Iraq during Operation Provide Comfort (1991).

He has also served in a civilian capacity on the Multinational Force-Iraq/U.S. Embassy Baghdad Joint Campaign Plan Assessment Team (2009) and as a consultant or advisor to the congressionally mandated Iraq Study Group (2006), the Multinational Corps-Iraq Information Operations Task Force (2005-2006), and the State Department's Future of Iraq defense policy working group (2002-2003). In 1992, he took a leave of absence from the Institute to work on the U.S. Air Force Gulf War Air Power Survey.

Mr. Eisenstadt earned an MA in Arab Studies from Georgetown University and has traveled widely in the Middle East. He speaks Arabic and Hebrew, and reads French.

DISCLOSURE FORM FOR WITNESSES
COMMITTEE ON ARMED SERVICES
U.S. HOUSE OF REPRESENTATIVES

INSTRUCTION TO WITNESSES: Rule 11, clause 2(g)(5), of the Rules of the U.S. House of Representatives for the 114th Congress requires nongovernmental witnesses appearing before House committees to include in their written statements a curriculum vitae and a disclosure of the amount and source of any federal contracts or grants (including subcontracts and subgrants), or contracts or payments originating with a foreign government, received during the current and two previous calendar years either by the witness or by an entity represented by the witness and related to the subject matter of the hearing. This form is intended to assist witnesses appearing before the House Committee on Armed Services in complying with the House rule. Please note that a copy of these statements, with appropriate redactions to protect the witness's personal privacy (including home address and phone number) will be made publicly available in electronic form not later than one day after the witness's appearance before the committee. Witnesses may list additional grants, contracts, or payments on additional sheets, if necessary.

Witness name: Michael Eisenstadt

Capacity in which appearing: (check one)

◉ Individual

◯ Representative

If appearing in a representative capacity, name of the company, association or other entity being represented: _____

Federal Contract or Grant Information: If you or the entity you represent before the Committee on Armed Services has contracts (including subcontracts) or grants (including subgrants) with the federal government, please provide the following information:

2015

Federal grant/ contract	Federal agency	Dollar value	Subject of contract or grant
Honorarium	U.S. Army	$500	Oral Presentation

2014

Federal grant/ contract	Federal agency	Dollar value	Subject of contract or grant
Please see attached supplement			

2013

Federal grant/ contract	Federal agency	Dollar value	Subject of contract or grant
Please see attached supplement			

Foreign Government Contract or Payment Information: If you or the entity you represent before the Committee on Armed Services has contracts or payments originating from a foreign government, please provide the following information:

2015

Foreign contract/ payment	Foreign government	Dollar value	Subject of contract or payment
Honorarium	U.A.E.	$1,225	Oral Presentation

2014

Foreign contract/ payment	Foreign government	Dollar value	Subject of contract or payment
Please see attached supplement			

2013

Foreign contract/ payment	Foreign government	Dollar value	Subject of contract or payment
Please see attached supplement			

American Enterprise Institute for Public Policy Research

Statement before the House Armed Services Committee
Subcommittee on Emerging Threats and Capabilities
"The Counterterrorism Strategy Against the Islamic State of Iraq and the Levant:
Are We on the Right Path?"

America's Strategy Against ISIS Must Focus on Assisting the Iraqi Security Forces and Government

Frederick W. Kagan

Christopher DeMuth Chair and Director, Critical Threats Project

American Enterprise Institute

June 24, 2015

Frederick W. Kagan
June 24, 2015

"There is no military solution to the problem" has become a constant refrain in American strategic and policy discourse, particularly as it relates to the Islamic State of Iraq and al Sham (ISIS). The refrain is, of course, a truism. The problem of ISIS transcends its military threat and requires a solution that is not purely military. That solution MUST have a military component, however, for the simple reason that this is a war. Observing that war is a complex, multi-faceted phenomenon that engages diplomacy, politics, economics, society, and many other things is one thing. Arguing that one can be successful in war without the effective use of military force is quite another. It will take more than diplomacy to defeat ISIS; it will also take fighting. The questions are: Who will do the fighting? What do they need to succeed? What role should the U.S. play? How would effective military strategy fit into a larger all-of-government and coalition strategy?

Iraq has a government, a functioning (if battered) military and police force, and a population mobilizing under the control of various leaders (including some Iranians) to fight ISIS. It is neither necessary nor wise for the U.S. to send large numbers of combat forces into Iraq to do the fighting themselves, and no one is suggesting that. Sound American strategy in Iraq must surely focus on enabling and assisting the legitimate security forces of the legitimate government of Iraq to defeat ISIS and re-establish the sovereignty of the Iraqi state.

The current administration strategy is correctly oriented on this approach, and suggestions that the U.S. should abandon Baghdad and support an independent Kurdistan or Sunni Arab tribes in a way that might bring about an independent "Sunnistan" are misguided, for reasons I will explore momentarily. But the current strategy is not providing the kind and quantity of support required to succeed. It is not merely that it is under-resourced, although it is, but also that it misunderstands the nature of the assistance that the U.S. must give in order for Iraqis to succeed.

ISIS has developed into an extremely sophisticated and capable hybrid army, as the analysts at the Institute for the Study of War have articulated in detail.[1] It maneuvers mechanized formations in the field while simultaneously engaging in dispersed urban warfare, raids and ambushes, and straightforward terrorism. It has been conducting an assassination campaign against members of the Sunni Arab community whom it thinks might form the basis for a rebellion against it similar to the "Anbar Awakening" for many years. It operates both within the population and apart from the population, deriving popular support or tolerance partly from communal grievances and partly from the terror and oppression it imposes on the large mass of Sunni Arabs who do not agree with its worldview.

The Iraqi Government will have to address the grievances much better than it has done so far, as Chairman Dempsey and Secretary Carter, among others, recently testified.[2] But the Iraqi military, supported by the coalition, will have to defeat the army that ISIS now has in the field as well as the instruments of oppression it has deployed throughout the areas it controls. Those are military and security functions, and they require priority until they are completed. For there can be no hope of a political settlement or the resolution of grievances while the ISIS army is in the field and while those whose grievances must be redressed are under the terrorized thrall of this brutal foe.

The destruction of the mechanized forces of ISIS should be a relatively straightforward task for the U.S. military, which was designed, after all, to do precisely that against much more sophisticated enemies. It is difficult to understand why ISIS has been able to move formations of vehicles around a theater patrolled by coalition airpower, and that is a problem that should be rectified as quickly as possible.

Frederick W. Kagan
June 24, 2015

The challenge of driving ISIS from within urban centers and the population is more complex, of course, as it always has been. But if the current strategy seems to be constraining the effectiveness of airpower against ISIS vehicles beyond the battle zone, it is excessively focused on providing only or primarily airpower to this more complicated fight. Airpower can certainly help a great deal in defeating ISIS fighters entrenched in cities. It was invaluable in 2007-2009 in support of American, Iraqi, and coalition ground forces clearing entrenched al Qaeda in Iraq (AQI) fighters out of dense urban as well as rural terrain. Making airpower effective in this situation will require relaxing constraints on the risk of civilian casualties—it simply is not possible to operate effectively in an urban fight without expecting to cause some collateral damage. It also requires expanding the footprint of U.S. military personnel on the ground who can serve as Forward Air Controllers (FACs). FACs would both make the application of airpower more effective and mitigate some of the risk of civilian casualties in urban areas.

But the Iraqi Security Forces (ISF) need more than air support. Hollowed-out by years of politically-motivated purging under former Prime Minister Nuri al Maliki, stunned and shamed by the collapse of four divisions in the initial ISIS advance last year, battered by a year of brutal warfare since then, and buffeted by continued setbacks, the ISF needs partners on the ground. U.S. trainers must embed with Iraqi units, as Max Boot and many others have explained articulately.[3] They will have to fight with those units, since advisors who do not join their advisees in combat lose credibility and miss the opportunity to help when they are most needed. They should also be able to bring a fuller array of American asymmetric capabilities to bear, including artillery and helicopter aviation, that provides immediate and responsive fire support to Iraqi troops in combat and, in the case of artillery, continues to be effective even in bad weather.

American and coalition forces could bring other asymmetric capabilities to bear against ISIS if restrictions on force size, basing, and operating patterns were relaxed. Our special mission units (SMUs) can and should conduct frequent raids against ISIS leaders and staff positions in support of both offensive and defensive ISF operations. SMUs have demonstrated their ability to disrupt enemy operations repeatedly in both Afghanistan and Iraq at a very low cost in American lives. A more expansive American footprint would also allow U.S. forces to enhance ground-based intelligence, surveillance, and reconnaissance assets, facilitating the gathering of the intelligence needed both to support SMU operations and also to avoid surprise. A larger number of American advisors embedded with Iraqi headquarters at all echelons could facilitate communications, planning, intelligence analysis, and many other supporting functions essential to the effective prosecution of war. I will not try to detail here the specific force requirements for this kind of operation except to note that the total overall force needed is likely in the vicinity of 20,000 U.S. troops.

There are three meaningful objections to such a deployment. First, that it may fail and may simply drag the U.S. deeper into a quagmire. Second, that it would put U.S. forces in the position of fighting alongside of and supporting Iranian troops and proxies. Third, paradoxically, that it would lead the Iranians to attack American forces in Iraq.

Any military undertaking runs the risk of failure, and the situation in Iraq is parlous enough to make that risk high for virtually any course of action. Were the president to deploy forces as suggested above with the missions and authorities described only to see them fail, he (or she) would face the same choice President Obama faces today: change the strategy and resources allocated to fight ISIS or accept the high

Frederick W. Kagan
June 24, 2015

risk of a permanent ISIS state. Stephen Walt has recently argued precisely for accepting the existence of an ISIS state rather than engaging in a major escalation.[4] But his argument is based on a series of misrepresentations about the threat ISIS poses to the West (in addition to a tendency toward moral equivalency between this genocidal organization and, for example, the British).

If it were true that ISIS could mobilize and radicalize only a relatively small number of people and could not meaningfully dispatch them to the West in support of widespread terrorist attacks, then the morally-repugnant realist argument for containment might make some sense. But ISIS has mobilized many thousands of foreigners in a process that continues to accelerate. Growing numbers of them are returning to the states of the West not exclusively, as Walt hopefully suggests, having turned away from the excesses of ISIS, but rather, at least in some cases, with the hope of bringing jihad to us. The argument for containment misses the most fundamental problem, in fact, by ignoring the reality that containment in this case means constant vicious sectarian warfare. It is precisely that sectarian warfare that is helping to radicalize and mobilize elements of the Muslim population around the world. Allowing it to persist indefinitely would pose an unacceptable level of risk to Americans here at home.

It is very difficult to make a sensible, fact-based case for the feasibility of containment of an ISIS state. It is therefore difficult to sustain policy recommendations that accept the serious risk that ISIS will be able to sustain itself. It is conceivable that things might reach such a point that only a massive American direct intervention would be sufficient to prevent that from occurring, but we are by no means yet at that point. It behooves us to do everything we can to avoid getting to that point, in fact. From which it follows that providing much more robust support to the Iraqi forces now in the field is by far the best option we can now choose.

The mutually-contradictory arguments about Iran merit consideration. Empowering Iran to control Iraq would be disastrous both for the fight against ISIS and for U.S. interests broadly. The Iranian government repeatedly and explicitly describes the goal of its strategy as expelling the United States from the region entirely and establishing a Persian hegemony (Tehran speaks of its "leadership") in its place. That prospect should be enough to end any discussion about simply backing Iran in Iraq. If it is not, however, we must reflect on the role that Iran and its proxies have been and are playing in this struggle. Despite lofty pan-Islamist rhetoric, the Iranian regime is defined by a powerful Shi'a identity and overwhelmingly supports sectarian Shi'a groups throughout the region. Those groups, in turn, have played central roles in persuading Sunni communities in Iraq and Syria that they face an existential threat that could require them to turn to ISIS or any other group that promises to protect them. Iranian-supported and Iranian-controlled forces, in other words, are major drivers of ISIS support and recruitment. Backing them will make the problem worse rather than better.

The trouble is that Iranian forces and proxies are now spread throughout Iraq and integrated with many Iraqi forces fighting ISIS. Recent reporting that U.S. forces will be sharing the base at Taqaddum in Anbar Province highlights the challenge of providing American assistance to the ISF without simultaneously empowering Iran.[5] It may be that Iranian influence is now so pervasive that it cannot be reduced or checked, but that proposition has not been tested. It is suspect, in fact, given the continued resentment Iraqi leaders privately express about Iranian control and the reality that Arab Iraqis are just not that open to domination by Persians.

Frederick W. Kagan
June 24, 2015

But the U.S. has not offered enough assistance to Iraq to make it a reasonable calculation for Iraqi Prime Minister Haider al Abadi to send the Iranians packing. The additional support suggested above should come with a demand—Iraqi units can have one set of advisors at a time. If they want the real asymmetric capabilities that American forces could bring if they were allowed to, then they have to send the Iranians away from those units. There is reason to believe that the Iraqis will make that choice if we put enough assistance on the table. Considering the downside risks of allowing the current situation to develop as it has been, it is well worth the attempt.

It is true that Iranian proxies could attack U.S. forces in Iraq (or elsewhere in the region) if Tehran chose to oppose an escalation of U.S. activity in Iraq in that way. And Iran's leaders might do so. They are observing the redeployment of American troops to Iraq with concern and are escalating their rhetoric about American support to ISIS (yes, they believe that) and America's intention to establish a permanent imperial base in Iraq from which to threaten Iran.[6] This hostile rhetoric is noteworthy as it comes in the context of the nuclear negotiations and of U.S. hints and suggestions that the White House sees Iran as a potential partner in Iraq.

The real question here, however, is simple: Is the U.S. prepared to give Ayatollah Khamenei veto power over our activities in the region? As long as there are any Americans in the Middle East, the Iranians have the ability to attack them. Yielding to the principle that such a risk means that the U.S. must never take action that might provoke Tehran will make the U.S. a de facto partner in its own expulsion from the region and the establishment of an Iranian hegemony. It does not follow, of course, that the U.S. should go out of its way to provoke Iran, since American interests are not served by a war with Iran in Iraq. But supporting the Iraqi military in defeating ISIS—another stated objective of Tehran—should not be enough to trigger an Iranian-sponsored attack on U.S. personnel. If it is, then the state of U.S.-Iranian relations is far worse than we have been led to believe and the idea of meaningful negotiations with such an implacable enemy is bizarre.

Some increasingly argue that the U.S. should abandon Baghdad and the decrepit Iraqi Security Forces largely or entirely and instead focus on helping the Kurds and/or the Sunni tribes directly. These ideas are superficially appealing. The Kurds are steadfast and determined enemies of ISIS and have been effective in holding it at bay and even pushing it back in some areas. The Sunni tribes, on the other hand, rose up against ISIS once in its previous incarnation as AQI, and one could hope that they would do so again.

The idea of victory through Kurdistan is problematic for at least two reasons, however. The first is geographical and strategic—Kurdistan is close to Mosul and ISIS-controlled areas of Ninewah, Kirkuk, and Diyala Provinces, but it is far from Anbar, Salahaddin, Baghdad, and Babil. Kurdish forces, suitably reinforced, might conceivably clear ISIS from regions along the Kurdish region's immediate borders, but could not clear it from its deep safe-havens nor drive it from the mixed-sectarian areas in which it seeks to thrive. And Kurdish leaders would never try to do so.

The second problem with the Kurdish solution is ethnic. Tensions between Arabs and Kurds all along the ethnic seam are running high. ISIS deliberately stokes those tensions, but the consolidation of Kurdish control over Kirkuk and other disputed areas causes many Sunni Arabs to fear that Kurdistan will ultimately engulf most of Mosul, much of Ninewah, Kirkuk, and parts of Diyala that they view as Arab. There is ample historical precedent to assess that these fears will lead to ethnic violence—indeed, there are some worrying indicators that they already are doing so. Arming the Kurds and facilitating Kurdish expansion into Arab areas in the name of chasing out ISIS is thus very likely to cause an ethnic war to explode against the background of the ongoing sectarian war.

Relying primarily on the Sunni tribes is problematic for different reasons. To begin with, as we have noted, ISIS is on to that trick. The terrorists have been selectively destroying all those they think could lead such an uprising. They may not have cowed the population or prevented other anti-ISIS leaders from emerging, but they have badly disrupted the social mechanisms that made the Anbar Awakening possible. Nor are the tribes currently organized into effective fighting forces, as they would have to be to take on the hybrid army that ISIS now fields. It will take a lot longer to train hordes of tribesmen—if they became suddenly available—to the necessary level of combat capability than it would take to train, advise, and assist the ISF while encouraging Sunni enrollment into that force.

Any such efforts, moreover, would deeply undermine the prospects for a political resolution to this crisis. Trying to work with Baghdad, the Sunni tribes, and the Kurds to reconcile their differences and address grievances within the context of an Iraqi state will certainly be difficult, even if an appropriate military solution to the military problem is found. Trying to facilitate a peaceful agreement between an independent Kurdistan, a newly-forming independent Sunnistan, and a rump Shiastan will be orders of magnitude more difficult.

There is no agreement between Kurds and Arabs about where the border between them should be, and their conflicting claims make any such agreement highly unlikely. It has been difficult enough to manage this problem within the context of a unified Iraq, which makes the issue of borders considerably less significant than it would be if there were to be two independent states. The history of efforts to mediate such disputes peacefully is not encouraging moreover—one need only consider the collapse of the Yugoslav state in the 1990s. Negotiating the emergence of an independent Kurdish state will also involve enormously complicated regional diplomacy, and could well alienate Turkey, a critical (if difficult and equivocal) partner in the struggle against ISIS in Syria.

The prospect of an independent Sunnistan is even more fraught. The Sunni Arab regions in Iraq, unlike the Kurds, have never had a notion of an independent Sunni Arab state. No one has seriously thought through what the boundaries of such a state would look like. Trying to help establish Sunnistan while also supporting Kurdish independence would immediately put the struggle for borders in Ninewah Province front and center, and would certainly distract from any efforts to fight ISIS. But Iraq's Sunnis are not remotely as cohesive as its Kurds. It is highly unlikely that there would emerge a single Sunnistan, or even a single Sunni federal region within Iraq. We are much more likely to see multiple Sunni Arab mini-states try to emerge, fighting each other, the Shia, and the Kurds for power, resources, and boundaries.

And, of course, we face the additional problem that ISIS currently controls most of Sunni Arab Iraq, while the Sunni tribes even with the support of the ISF and the coalition have been unable to retake it. The notion that the tribes alone, without the ISF, and while fighting amongst themselves and with their neighbors for political supremacy, could expel ISIS is implausible.

Frederick W. Kagan
June 24, 2015

If Iraqis choose over time to partition their state peacefully either within a federal paradigm or into independent states, the U.S. need not oppose them. But it is fully as wrong, imperialistic, and counter-productive to force the Iraqis to partition as it would be to occupy and govern Iraq ourselves.

Supporting the current Iraqi Security Forces with serious military assistance across the full spectrum of the asymmetric capabilities that the U.S. can provide is by far the least unattractive of the options facing us in the fight against ISIS in Iraq. The risks are high, and the costs may be high. But the alternative is accepting a major strategic defeat that will significantly increase the risk to the U.S. and European homelands, as well as fueling continued regional war.

---

[1] Jessica Lewis McFate, "The ISIS Defense in Iraq and Syria: Countering an Adaptive Enemy," *Institute for the Study of War*, Middle East Security Report 27, p.17, May 2015, http://www.understandingwar.org/sites/default/files/ISIS%20Defense%20in%20Iraq%20and%20Syria%20--%20Standard.pdf
[2] General Dempsey, "Testimony on US policy towards Iraq and Syria and the Threat Posed by the Islamic State of Iraq and the Levant," *US Senate Committee on Armed Services*, September 16, 2014, http://www.armed-services.senate.gov/imo/media/doc/14-66%20-%209-16-14.pdf and Secretary of Defense Ash Carter, "Statement on U.S. Policy and Strategy in the Middle East before the House Armed Services Committee," *U.S. Department of Defense*, June 17, 2015, http://www.defense.gov/Speeches/Speech.aspx?SpeechID=1949
[3] Max Boot and Jeane J. Kirkpatrick, "Defeating ISIS: Policy Innovation Memorandum No. 51," *Council on Foreign Relations*, November 14, 2014, http://www.cfr.org/iraq/defeating-isis/p33773
[4] "What Should the US Do About the Islamic State?" *PBS News Hour*, August 24, 2014. http://www.pbs.org/newshour/bb/u-s-islamic-state/
[5] David Alexander, "U.S. troops at Taqaddum to help Iraqis plan fight for Ramadi," *Reuters*, June 12, 2015, http://www.reuters.com/article/2015/06/12/us-mideast-crisis-usa-taqaddum-idUSKBN0OS1DI20150612
[6] "Didar nokhost vazir iraq ba rahbar enqelab" [Iraqi prime minister's visit with the leader of the revolution], Preservation and Publication Office of Ayatollah Seyyed Ali Khamenei, June 17, 2015, http://farsi.khamenei.ir/news-content?id=29974.

Dr. Frederick W. Kagan
Christopher DeMuth Chair and Director, Critical Threats Project
American Enterprise Institute

Frederick W. Kagan, author of the 2007 report Choosing Victory: A Plan for Success in Iraq, is one of the intellectual architects of the successful "surge" strategy in Iraq. He is the director of AEI's Critical Threats Project and a former professor of military history at the U.S. Military Academy at West Point. His books range from Lessons for a Long War (AEI Press, 2010), coauthored with Thomas Donnelly, to the End of the Old Order: Napoleon and Europe, 1801-1805 (Da Capo, 2006).

Experience
Associate Professor of Military History, 2001-2005; Assistant Professor of Military History, 1995-2001; U.S. Military Academy at West Point

Education
Ph.D., Russian and Soviet military history;
B.A., Soviet and East European studies, Yale University

DISCLOSURE FORM FOR WITNESSES
COMMITTEE ON ARMED SERVICES
U.S. HOUSE OF REPRESENTATIVES

INSTRUCTION TO WITNESSES: Rule 11, clause 2(g)(5), of the Rules of the U.S. House of Representatives for the 114th Congress requires nongovernmental witnesses appearing before House committees to include in their written statements a curriculum vitae and a disclosure of the amount and source of any federal contracts or grants (including subcontracts and subgrants), or contracts or payments originating with a foreign government, received during the current and two previous calendar years either by the witness or by an entity represented by the witness and related to the subject matter of the hearing. This form is intended to assist witnesses appearing before the House Committee on Armed Services in complying with the House rule. Please note that a copy of these statements, with appropriate redactions to protect the witness's personal privacy (including home address and phone number) will be made publicly available in electronic form not later than one day after the witness's appearance before the committee. Witnesses may list additional grants, contracts, or payments on additional sheets, if necessary.

Witness name: Frederick W. Kagan

Capacity in which appearing: (check one)

◉ Individual

◯ Representative

If appearing in a representative capacity, name of the company, association or other entity being represented: NA

Federal Contract or Grant Information: If you or the entity you represent before the Committee on Armed Services has contracts (including subcontracts) or grants (including subgrants) with the federal government, please provide the following information:

2015

Federal grant/ contract	Federal agency	Dollar value	Subject of contract or grant
Please see attached supplement			

2014

Federal grant/ contract	Federal agency	Dollar value	Subject of contract or grant
Please see attached supplement			

2013

Federal grant/ contract	Federal agency	Dollar value	Subject of contract or grant
Please see attached supplement			

Foreign Government Contract or Payment Information: If you or the entity you represent before the Committee on Armed Services has contracts or payments originating from a foreign government, please provide the following information:

2015

Foreign contract/ payment	Foreign government	Dollar value	Subject of contract or payment
Please see attached supplement			

2014

Foreign contract/ payment	Foreign government	Dollar value	Subject of contract or payment
Please see attached supplement			

2013

Foreign contract/ payment	Foreign government	Dollar value	Subject of contract or payment
Please see attached supplement			

Prepared Testimony to the House Armed Services Committee, Subcommittee on Emerging Threats and Capabilities

The Next Decade: Aligning Strategy Against the Islamic State

Brian Fishman
Counterterrorism Research Fellow
International Studies Program, New America

June 24, 2015

Chairman Wilson and Ranking Member Langevin, Members of the Committee, thank you for inviting me here today for a discussion of ISIS.

The Islamic State's Goals and Operational Vectors

The Islamic State is a hybrid organization that aims to establish an extremely harsh form of Islamic law across much of the world. It has five basic operational vectors to advance that goal:

- Establishing a proto-state, including the bureaucratic framework for governance;
- Waging military campaigns in Iraq and Syria, including the use of terrorist tactics to suppress dissent and intimidate enemies;
- Encouraging followers to independently attack hostile governments, including in the West;
- Building a network of affiliates working to establish jihadi-styled governance around the world, notably in North Africa, Yemen, and Afghanistan;
- Inspiring jihadis around the world to either join the organization or at least endorse its vision of a future Caliphate.

Critically, the Islamic State's fundamental goal and its basic operational vectors—with the exception of building an affiliate network and expanding core operations to Syria—have been relatively consistent since October 2006. That is when the Islamic State of Iraq was founded out of the institutional framework of al-Qaeda in Iraq.

We do not often recognize our long history fighting ISIS, but we have effectively been fighting the group—under slightly different names—for nearly a decade. And, I am sorry to say, it is likely going to require at least another decade of sustained national effort to defeat this organization.

The Last Decade of War Against ISIS and its Predecessors

From 2006 to 2008, we fought ISIS effectively, but failed to destroy it. The "surge" of 150,000 American troops into Iraq, including crucial special operators, and a concerted effort to inspire the Awakening of Sunni tribes against the Islamic State of Iraq eliminated its ability to control territory and forced it to abandon large-scale conventional military operations.

Nonetheless, the group was never defeated. The Islamic State of Iraq remained one of the deadliest terrorist groups in the world; was continually viewed by jihadis globally as the kernel of a future Caliphate; maintained a strong presence near Mosul, Iraq and in Syrian border areas; established the bureaucratic structure for future 'governance'; and sustained the ability to play spoiler in Iraqi politics by assassinating hostile Sunnis and using terrorist attacks to encourage the Shia-dominated Maliki government into embracing its sectarian tendencies.

There are some key lessons from this era that we should remember today:

1. ISIS is vulnerable to military pressure; despite its growth, the group's conventional military power is limited.
2. ISIS is extremely resilient and can shift its geographic base of operations and mode of organization relatively quickly.
3. Operational setbacks impact ISIS' global appeal, but the group will remain a viable Caliphate to its supporters so long as it controls territory and continues to fight.
4. Even a diminished ISIS can operate as a political spoiler in both Iraq and Syria.

The Islamic State of Iraq survived by shifting its geographic focus and mode of operation—and then waiting for Iraqi political conditions to shift and U.S. focus on the group to wane. The most important lesson here for U.S. policymakers is that our future strategy must be sustainable. A scramble for short-term operational wins is insufficient.

The Next Decade of War Against ISIS

ISIS will not be defeated so long as the Syrian civil war continues and Sunnis in Iraq live in mortal fear of their own government. Military action can contain ISIS and limit its ability to control territory and people, but such gains will be inadequate—and fleeting—without political resolutions in Syria and Iraq.

The ugly reality is that the United States does not have policy levers to defeat the Islamic State in the near term without massive and politically untenable intervention in both Iraq and Syria. This is going to be a long fight and our strategy must be calibrated such that it is sustainable.

Rather than scope an entire strategy, which would include many of the basic operations we are undertaking today, I will address some of the key questions we face currently and lay out the conditions under which our approach should change dramatically:

- Should the United States support Syrian rebels focused on deposing Assad in addition to those focused on destroying ISIS?
    - Yes. Although this approach carries significant risks, such as increased Iranian troublemaking and weapons falling into jihadi hands, it will bolster relations with Turkey and increase pressure on the Assad regime to accept political compromise. The United States should not under any circumstances legitimize al-Qaeda-linked jihadi groups like Jabhat al-Nusrah, as some of our Arab allies seem to want.

- Should the United States continue to funnel weapons through Baghdad to Kurdish and Sunni factions fighting ISIS?
    - Yes, for now. ISIS will not be destroyed unless Sunnis in Iraq feel secure from their own government, but Baghdad remains the most important force for stability in Iraq. We should circumvent the government only if fundamentally redefining political authority in Iraq is the end-state we seek. That may become necessary, and it should remain an option on the table, but it should be a last resort.

- Should the United States increase the number of U.S. troops on the ground in Iraq?
    - Moderately increasing the number of troops in Iraq may improve our operational outcomes, but it will not lead to the destruction of ISIS. If 150,000 American troops could not destroy the Islamic State of Iraq seven years ago, why would 1/10th that number have lasting success against what is today a much stronger foe? A mini-surge can push ISIS into a box, but that box will remain large enough to pose a major strategic threat.
    - Moreover, a significant increase in U.S. troops on the ground will provide ISIS a meaningful propaganda boost globally and increases the risk of lone-wolf attacks in the west. It also increases the risk of strikes on U.S. troops by Iranian-backed militias.

Our decade of war against ISIS has not produced a decisive outcome, in large measure because our strategy and commitment has been inconsistent. To be successful in the next decade, we must have a clear, consistent, and sustainable strategy. Fortunately, Jihadi organizations have a long track record of self-destruction—and ISIS is laying the seeds of its own defeat by creating more enemies than even it can kill. But unless we resolve the basic political challenges in Iraq and Syria, ISIS will persist.

Mr. Brian Fishman
Counterterrorism Research Fellow, International Studies Program
New America Foundation

Brian Fishman is a Counterterrorism Research Fellow at the New America Foundation and a Research Fellow with the Combating Terrorism Center (CTC) at West Point. He previously served as the CTC's Director of Research and was a professor in the Department of Social Sciences at West Point. Fishman was a regular contributor to the CTC's Harmony Project reports; he authored Dysfunction and Decline: Lessons Learned from Inside al-Qa`ida in Iraq, co-authored al-Qa`ida's Foreign Fighters in Iraq: A First Look at the Sinjar Records, and edited Bombers, Bank Accounts, and Bleedout: al-Qa`ida's Road In and Out of Iraq. As part of his CENTCOM Assessment Team. Fishman was a founding editor of the CTC Sentinel.

Before joining the CTC in 2005, Fishman was the Foreign Affairs/Defense Legislative Assistant for Congresswoman Lynn Woolsey (CA-6). He worked extensively on the Middle East peace process, proliferation, Chinese human rights, and landmine and UXO cleanup. Fishman has published in the Washington Quarterly, the Annals of the American Academy of Political and Social Science, and numerous edited volumes.

Fishman has appeared in numerous national and international media outlets, including The New York Times, The Washington Post, PBS' Bill Moyers Journal, National Public Radio, NBC Nightly News, and Fox News. He holds a Masters in International Affairs (MIA) from Columbia University and a B.A. from the University of California Los Angeles.

QUESTIONS SUBMITTED BY MEMBERS POST HEARING

JUNE 24, 2015

QUESTIONS SUBMITTED BY MR. WILSON

Mr. WILSON. In your testimony, you call the suggestion of abandoning the central government in Baghdad and arming the Kurds and/or Sunni tribes directly as "superficially appealing." Can you provide us with more detail on why arming and supporting the Kurds directly to fight Daesh is bad for our overall strategy?

Dr. KAGAN. The Kurds cannot and should not fight ISIS beyond their ethnic boundaries. They have very little ability to project power outside of their home areas—their military forces are primarily designed for self-defense—and their military activities in Arab lands have repeatedly called forth violent responses and fueled recruitment for al Qaeda in Iraq and ISIS. Arabs in Ninewah, Kirkuk, and Diyala Provinces traditionally view Kurdish incursions into what they regard as "Arab" lands as provocations intended to annex those lands to a greater Kurdistan and conduct ethnic cleansing to Kurdify them. The Kurds fuel these fears somewhat by prominently displaying maps of "Kurdistan" that show it lapping over into disputed areas and through various other activities and statements. I offer no opinion on how control of the disputed territories along the KRG border should be resolved, other than it should be resolved peacefully. I take no position on the historical rights of any group to that land. Nor do I accuse the Kurds of seeking to seize more land than might rightfully be regarded as theirs, still less of intending to conduct ethnic cleansing. But the perception among many Arab communities in these areas is different, and, from the standpoint of strategy, only that perception matters. Kurdish forces operating for an extended time in Arab areas of Iraq will generate ethnic violence that, in turn, will create conditions for the resilience of ISIS as a defender of the Arabs. The Kurds cannot, then, help defeat ISIS other than by holding their own boundaries, which they should be assisted to do.

Mr. WILSON. You also indicate the importance of an inclusive Iraqi Army to counter the hollow force under previous Iraqi leader, yet the Iraqi Army has been unable to advance against Mosul and were not successful in maintaining control of Ramadi. What actions should the U.S. take to ensure that the Iraqi government continues to strengthen its central military for successful combat against ISIL?

Dr. KAGAN. The U.S. should increase its direct advice and assistance to the Iraqi Security Forces by embedding trainers, advisers, and forward air controllers with Iraqi Security Forces units; by deploying the full array of U.S. intelligence-gathering, analysis, and dissemination capabilities into Iraq; by providing significantly increased fixed- and rotary-wing aviation support, both attack and transport, to the ISF; by providing artillery support as necessary; and by deploying Quick Reaction Forces to protect the more dispersed U.S. footprint in extremis. The U.S. should simultaneously insist that any ISF units receiving such assistance reject and abjure assistance from Iranian security forces and the militias they control (specifically KH, AAH, and Badr). In a period of extremely low oil prices and, therefore, budgetary crisis in Baghdad, the U.S. should consider providing financial assistance to support the ISF as well.

––––––––

QUESTIONS SUBMITTED BY MR. LANGEVIN

Mr. LANGEVIN. Our comprehensive strategy to combat ISIL includes undercutting their flow of resources. Shutting down access to revenue, and closing the means by which funds flow to and from ISIL is a critical component of that strategy. The Department of Defense, the Department of State, the Department of the Treasury, the Department of Justice, and other intelligence and national security agencies all play a role in identifying and restricting ISIL's access to revenue, and revenue flows. I am interested to hear your thoughts on the effectiveness of the actions we are taking with respect to counter-threat financing, the role the DOD plays in identifying networks and informing those decisions, the threshold for an organization to receive our attention with respect to terrorist financing action, and given the current environment, should that strategy and threshold being revisited? Would you say that counter-threat financing efforts are a primary, secondary or tertiary concern of our military and intel community? Finally, how effective have our economic pressures been to date and what is your assessment of the ISIL Counter-Financing Working Group?

Ms. ROBINSON. I thank Ranking Member Langevin for this important question. The short answer is that counter-threat financing efforts have lagged other aspects of the counter-ISIL effort. One reason is that the Counter-ISIL Financing Working Group has been formed relatively recently. A mechanism for reporting progress on a periodic basis, as well as assessments to ascertain whether the current approach is effective, would be advisable. Another, more fundamental reason is a shortage of ground-based intelligence due to our current mode of operating and our shortage of intelligence assets. Generating robust and reliable intelligence flows is essential for this line of effort to yield results. There is a need for greater intelligence both inside the Iraq-Syria main theater of operations for ISIL as well as internationally. Since the largest sources of funding are internal, increasing intelligence about funding activities inside Iraq and Syria would be the logical priority. Most analysis currently suggests that internal sources of revenue are more important to sustaining ISIL than outside resources, such as donations from benefactors in other countries. That is to say, revenues from extortion of the Iraqi and Syrian population, illicit oil and gas smuggling, and sale of looted antiquities are considered to be major sources of ISIL funding at this time. Therefore, the priority for the counter-threat financing line of operations should be to gain precise real-time information about how the internal funding networks operate and to identify the node in that network where resource generation can most efficiently and effectively be disrupted and dismantled. The computers and communications devices seized in the May 2015 raid by U.S. special operations forces in eastern Syria that killed Abu Sayyaf, a senior member of ISIL's leadership cadre, yielded highly useful information about the organization's current illicit oil, gas, and financial organizations. Furthermore, the analysis from the computers and communications devices seized in that raid is ongoing, and that work will significantly enhance the U.S. government's understanding of how ISIL is operating today. Based on the research I have done on ISIL and on special operations forces, the importance of capturing such data and ISIL leaders and facilitators who can yield important current intelligence cannot be overstated. Certainly, vital intelligence can be gathered through remote technical means, but ISIL's (and other terrorist) leaders have grown increasingly savvy about protecting their communications and information. Therefore, when such targets present themselves, the objective should be to capture them, if at all possible, whether by U.S. or other forces, so that the intelligence can be collected and analyzed. This ultimately contributes far more toward achieving the strategic goal of degrading and defeating ISIL than airstrikes that kill individual leaders and facilitators but yield no intelligence dividend. Those leaders and facilitators can be replaced with relative ease. ISIL will not be defeated unless the United States and its partners shift to an intelligence-driven war. This is one important change in priority in how the war is fought that I would recommend. External resources also matter, of course. Two member states of the counter-ISIL coalition, Italy and Saudi Arabia, have agreed to lead a working group focused on this issue along with the United States. Within the U.S. government, the Treasury Department and the National Counterterrorism Center are the lead entities for pursuing counter-threat finance efforts aimed at both internal and external resources fueling ISIL. The coalition's Counter-ISIL Financing Working Group was formed relatively recently, as noted, and a detailed report card on its efforts would be extremely helpful. Finally, the role of Turkey as a conduit for illicit trade has been widely reported. The importance of stopping flows of goods and funds through that major transit point cannot be overstated. Turkey's agreement to allow armed airstrikes against ISIL from bases on its territory may be a hopeful sign that further progress on cross-border flows can be made in the remainder of the year. A final note regarding the understanding of ISIL financing networks. Historical information is useful, and can serve to identify previous networks, facilitators and financiers that might still be active. RAND has conducted analysis of documents captured from ISIL's predecessor organization, al Qaeda in Iraq, as well as research on currently active networks.*

Mr. LANGEVIN. Ms. Robinson, I believe an effective strategy must be a coordinated, well thought out whole-of-government effort. You recently returned from Jordan and Iraq and noted the lack of coordination between the U.S. lines of effort,

---

* See testimony on this subject by RAND political scientists Seth Jones (''Breaking the Bank: Testimony presented before the House Financial Services Committee, Task Force to Investigate Terrorist Financing,'' April 22, 2015) and Patrick B. Johnston (''Countering ISIL's Financing: Testimony Presented Before the House Financial Services Committee on November 13, 2014,'' Santa Monica, Calif.: RAND Corporation, CT–419, November 2014).

and even more concerning, a lack of consensus on the number of lines of effort. In your opinion, how can these disconnects be addressed to unify the U.S. strategy?

Ms. ROBINSON. Inadequate unity of effort plagues every level of this war, and it will cripple the coalition unless it is remedied. At the highest level, no single synchronizer of U.S. government efforts has been named. U.S. government departments or agencies are designated the leads for one of the nine lines of effort, but there is no daily orchestration of the campaign in a whole-of-government or whole-of-coalition sense. The White House is coordinating policy deliberations and decisions, but no entity has been charged with coordinating operations across the lines of effort and conducting periodic assessments. Possible models include an interagency task force or a czar, such as the Special Representative for Afghanistan and Pakistan. This coordination work could be done with a dedicated staff in the White House, but it might distract the latter from its proper focus on policy and strategy, as opposed to implementation. The U.S. military describes the effort as having nine lines, while the White House and the State Department have described it as having four or five; this is indicative, at a very superficial but important level, of a government that is not speaking or thinking with one voice. A great deal more thought should be given to the nature of ISIL, now that we understand it is not going to disappear quickly, and from that fashion the right strategy and the right architecture. Given the complexity of the Iraq-Syria theater and the emergence of a significant network of ISIL affiliates, a division of labor between those two efforts might make sense. Within the Iraq-Syria theater, greater effort could be made to ensure that strategic, operational, and tactical actions across those two countries are synchronized. The Department of Defense leads two of the nine lines of effort, but the three-star command in charge of both Iraq and Syria, the Combined Joint Task Force–Operation Inherent Resolve, has not been fully staffed, according to the joint manning document. That suggests a lack of commitment to enable this primary warfighting command. I understand that that the Combined Joint Interagency Task Force–Syria has struggled mightily to gain the requested staff. Also, those two commands are not co-located—they are based in two different countries in the region—which creates an additional burden to foster a one-theater and one-team mentality. While in Iraq, I detected frictions between the military commands and the U.S. embassy, with the trainers and advisers clamoring for equipment but the security-assistance office unable to make the U.S. system work quickly enough to meet all of the needs. I also noted an unclear division of labor on the critical tribal engagement effort and the equally critical information operations effort. There is also an unfortunate reversal in the unity of effort that was achieved within the special operations community, which reached a high point in Afghanistan. These examples illustrate the variety of areas where our own command and control and unity of effort could be improved. Finally, the most distressing phenomenon I have observed is a tendency to make even tactical decisions at very high levels of the U.S. government, rather than entrusting highly qualified officers and civilian officials to make decisions at the speed the war demands. The delegation of appropriate authority to lower echelons—what the U.S. military calls "mission command"—should be closely examined to document what I believe to be an enormous gap between doctrine and actual practice and the inefficiencies and ineffectiveness that results. The reason underlying this reluctance to delegate authority is presumably an aversion to risk. Failure is part of war and casualties are part of war; any well-trained officer and official will seek to minimize risk, but at this juncture we may be minimizing risk to forces and maximizing risk to mission.

Mr. LANGEVIN. What should be the United States' role in fighting Islamic extremism, and what should be the roles of regional actors? Does the U.S. government possess the right tools to fight an ideological war, including information operations authorities? What more should our allies be doing to counter Islamic extremism?

Ms. ROBINSON. In my view, the most effective voices in the struggle against Islamic extremism are Muslim voices. In addition, however, a particular subset may have even greater sway over those youths that are being attracted to ISIL's ranks. That subset is former ISIL fighters who deserted once they came into contact with the reality of the movement and its depravity. Family members and friends who have seen the toll taken on their loved ones provide another source of immediate, graphic testimony that can compete—in visceral, emotional terms—with the terrorist recruiters. The sophistication of this recruitment effort has been documented by an increasing number of enterprising journalists and other enterprises. The U.S. Congress has shown a great interest in this informational side of irregular warfare, which is the type of warfare that is in fact most common, and which the United States must make a commitment to understanding and grappling with. The United States can play an important role in understanding, devising, and funding effective information operations, even if the most effective voices in the actual operations are likely to be non- U.S. voices. The first step to effective information operations is achieving a deep understanding of the phenomenon. Much of the relevant discourse is now occurring on social media, and RAND has developed tools and methods to analyze large volumes of social media messages and derive operational insights from them. Understanding the conversation is only the first step; engaging effectively in that conversation is the next step, which is the current urgent need. We must also be able to understand what is in fact effective or ineffective, and for that more rigorous and meaningful impact measures are also sorely needed. The authorities issue has been tendentious. I recall many battalion commanders who lamented that they could call in a bomb strike but not issue a press release. For many years the U.S. government has been engaged in an internal bureaucratic and intellectual struggle over who within the U.S. government should be in charge of what type of information operations and how they should be conducted. This plays out in a given country between U.S. embassies and military commands, and at the Washington interdepartmental level. The easy default position is to call for the re-creation of the U.S. Information Agency, but this may not be the appropriate model for this era given social and technological changes. An independent commission could study this issue—without regard to bureaucratic equities—and propose policy changes and, if necessary, legislative action to ensure that the United States adequately grapples with this central front in today's irregular conflicts. From a military perspective, military information support operations units currently have the authority to support other countries' MISO capacity-building and conduct their own activities in the counter-terrorism realm, subject to the support of specific geographic combatant commands and U.S. chiefs of mission. What they most need is support to carry out those programs at a high-level of quality (in both substantive and technical terms) and to develop empirically-grounded measures of effectiveness. This is a vastly under-resourced part of the special operations community. Among the specific technical needs are cyber expertise, regional and historical expertise, marketing and branding expertise, and a case study repository to create a body of knowledge for this nascent field. The U.S. State Department has been making a serious effort to develop an effective approach to counter-messaging and online engagement, but this is just one aspect of influence and information operations. As part of this work, other countries' efforts at de-radicalization programs should be closely studied to learn what has and has not worked and why, so that a body of knowledge on best practices can be developed and shared.† This knowledge can be brought to bear in the Middle East through willing states, nongovernmental organizations, and international institutions. A particularly vulnerable population is the youth among the millions of refugees and displaced people in Iraq, Syria, Lebanon, Jordan, and Turkey. The tragedy of today will only be compounded and extended if the next generation of young people are lured into this way of life.

Mr. LANGEVIN. How should the United States define and approach the threat of Islamic extremism?

Ms. ROBINSON. Purveyors of violent Islamic extremism employ a distorted version of Islam to attract militants to a cause that seeks to undermine established governments, strike Western targets, and impose a draconian medieval type of rule backed by vicious, wanton violence. There is a debate over the correct terminology to use to define Islamic extremism. On one hand, some are wary to avoid antagonizing adherents to a faith, Islam, and unintentionally stimulating sympathy for or converts to violent forms of extreme Salafism or Wahhabism. On the other hand, some object to the anodyne term ''violent extremist organization,'' in that it does not specifically call out the use made of Islam to sway individuals into the path of violent jihad, senseless brutality, and, in the case of ISIL, nearly limitless atrocities carried out against both Muslim and non-Muslim alike. Not all violent extremists are Muslims, of course, and it is important to note the many stimulants and rationales that can be used in an effort to justify violent extremism and attract recruits. It is likely that approaches to dealing with various forms of violent extremism will differ. It is imperative, given the powerful attraction that groups like ISIL appear to hold over young and disaffected people in many countries, that specific measures be developed to address the phenomenon of violent Islamic extremism. The terrorist tactics that ISIL and other similar groups are using draw specifically, if erroneously, upon elements of the Islamic faith, its teachings, and its history to advance the organizations' ends, which are ultimately about power, not religion. The need to combat the distortion of Islam and attack the credibility of these organizations requires acknowledgement of the use being made of Islam and a superior knowledge of its true

---

† See, for example, research conducted by RAND senior political scientist Kim Cragin: ''Resisting Violent Extremism: A Conceptual Model for Non-Radicalization,'' Terrorism and Political Violence, Vol. 26, No. 2, 2014.

teachings. This is, to some degree, a struggle within Islam—particularly Sunni Islam—and those members of that faith have every reason to lead the effort to debunk, discredit, and defeat those who would tarnish the name of a religion embraced by millions of peaceloving people around the world.

Mr. LANGEVIN. What are the risks and/or trade-offs in how U.S. policy and strategy defines and addressed the nature of the Islamic extremism threat?

Ms. ROBINSON. As noted in my previous answer, a key risk is taking actions that prove counterproductive by actually stimulating greater support for terrorism, including additional converts to the ranks of fighters or self-radicalized individual attackers. A particular risk is creating a large and long-term footprint of U.S. military forces that terrorist groups can depict as invaders or occupiers. This can turn the focus away from the reality that most victims of Islamic extremist violence are, in fact, Muslims. One problem is that, within the U.S. military, the art of supporting others in the fight against terrorism is still insufficiently developed. Another problem is that many potential partners are also very weak and lack reliable capabilities that can be leveraged by the United States. Partnering cannot likely be reduced to a science, as there are many complex factors that will determine a good partner, the right conditions, and the degree and type of U.S. assistance that will enable a given partner to combat the terrorist threat in a credible and effective manner. But rigorous study and refined methods can certainly improve upon "U.S. partnering" and working "by, with, and through" other countries, as the U.S. Special Forces like to say. This approach and preference to support and work through other countries is now enshrined in U.S. National Security Strategy, U.S. National Military Strategy, and funded initiatives such as the Counter-Terrorism Partnership Fund. But not enough attention has been devoted to refining our partnership approaches, especially in the most common circumstances, where all available partners are flawed in some way yet, at the end of the day, are most likely a preferable primary actor to the U.S. soldier—at least in great numbers. This approach to warfare has not yet been elevated to the central position in U.S. military thinking, organization, doctrine, and personnel training and development that will be necessary for the United States to become truly adept in this realm. My own research for the special operations community has focused on deep study of their experiences in this realm, and on linking the tactical, operational, and strategic aspects of partnering in both concept and practice. One study outlines steps for improved interagency and special operations–conventional competence, as well as continued funding for those coordinating and training bodies developed over the past 13 years.‡

Mr. LANGEVIN. Our comprehensive strategy to combat ISIL includes undercutting their flow of resources. Shutting down access to revenue, and closing the means by which funds flow to and from ISIL is a critical component of that strategy. The Department of Defense, the Department of State, the Department of the Treasury, the Department of Justice, and other intelligence and national security agencies all play a role in identifying and restricting ISIL's access to revenue, and revenue flows. I am interested to hear your thoughts on the effectiveness of the actions we are taking with respect to counter-threat financing, the role the DOD plays in identifying networks and informing those decisions, the threshold for an organization to receive our attention with respect to terrorist financing action, and given the current environment, should that strategy and threshold being revisited? Would you say that counter-threat financing efforts are a primary, secondary or tertiary concern of our military and intel community? Finally, how effective have our economic pressures been to date and what is your assessment of the ISIL Counter-Financing Working Group?

Mr. EISENSTADT. I do not know the answer to all of your questions, but it is my understanding that counter threat financing is a primary concern of our military and intelligence community, because ISIL can't fight or govern without money, and because this is something that we can get our arms around, to some extent, and effect in a tangible way (unlike efforts to counter ISIL's appeal, which is a much more daunting task). My understanding is that we have had substantial success in diminishing ISIL's oil income, but ISIL's main sources of income are from taxes and criminal activities such as extortion, kidnap for ransom, and the sale of stolen goods (including archeological treasures). Coalition activities have not affected these sources of income.

Mr. LANGEVIN. What should be the United States' role in fighting Islamic extremism, and what should be the roles of regional actors? Does the U.S. government possess the right tools to fight an ideological war, including information operations

‡Linda Robinson, Paul D. Miller, John Gordon IV, Jeffrey Decker, Michael Schwille, and Raphael S. Cohen, Improving Strategic Competence: Lessons from 13 Years of War, Santa Monica, Calif.: RAND Corporation, RR–816–A, 2014.

authorities? What more should our allies be doing to counter Islamic extremism? [Question #7, for cross-reference.]

Mr. EISENSTADT. The U.S. should play the role of enabler of its regional partners, as this is likely to be a decades-long struggle, and the U.S. needs to husband its resources, and build capacity among its regional partners so that any military victory is lasting. The U.S. could send 50,000 troops into Iraq and defeat ISIL in relatively short order and at some cost, but unless the politics of our allies change, and they develop an autonomous capacity to ensure internal security, ISIL will regenerate in 3–5 years and all this would be for naught. As for the ability of the U.S. government to fight an ideological war, I believe that we are neither framing the issue correctly, nor are we fighting it correctly. Various U.S. government documents talk about countering ISIL's ideology, countering its narrative, or exposing its hypocrisy, true nature, or false claims of acting in the name of religion. ISIL's appeal is only partly religious or ideological, and by overemphasizing this component, the USG seems to be overlooking the many other reasons that people join ISIL. And it is not clear how the military campaign against ISIL is tied to this effort to undermine ISIL's appeal. It seems that the two should be closely linked. So the U.S. seems to lack a proper understanding of how to prosecute this central element of the campaign against ISIL, and how all the elements of its counter-ISIL campaign contribute to this effort. In my mind, undermining ISIL's appeal should be the decisive line of operation of our campaign. But it is consistently listed as number six of our nine lines of effort.

Mr. LANGEVIN. How should the United States define and approach the threat of Islamic extremism?

Mr. EISENSTADT. I would defer to my colleagues who specialize in this issue, though I would say that it depends on the context. In the United States, the emphasis should probably be on education, focusing on an individual's social connections, and preventing peer radicalization and recruitment via face-to-face and social media contacts. In the Middle East, the answer lies in defusing the conflicts in Syria, Iraq, and elsewhere that have driven the radicalization process, though it will be very hard to deal with the radicalization process in Europe and the U.S., without addressing its root causes in the Middle East. So the two are linked.

Mr. LANGEVIN. What are the risks and/or trade-offs in how U.S. policy and strategy defines and addressed the nature of the Islamic extremism threat?

Mr. EISENSTADT. By pursuing a long-war strategy, as I recommended in response to question 7 [see above], there is a risk that the extremist threat will metastasize before the U.S. effort gains momentum. Indeed, the longer that ISIL and groups like it survive efforts to defeat them, the greater their appeal is likely to be. To win, they simply have to avoid defeat, and they have been doing much better than that. This is in effect what seems to be happening. And the U.S. does not seem to have successfully linked its military operations and its efforts to undermine ISIL's appeal. As a result, it has accepted defeats in Ramadi and elsewhere with relatively equanimity, stating that they are only tactical setbacks, whereas these battlefield victories for ISIL only feed its myth of invincibility, and are seen by ISIL and its supports as strategic victories.

Mr. LANGEVIN. Our comprehensive strategy to combat ISIL includes undercutting their flow of resources. Shutting down access to revenue, and closing the means by which funds flow to and from ISIL is a critical component of that strategy. The Department of Defense, the Department of State, the Department of the Treasury, the Department of Justice, and other intelligence and national security agencies all play a role in identifying and restricting ISIL's access to revenue, and revenue flows. I am interested to hear your thoughts on the effectiveness of the actions we are taking with respect to counter-threat financing, the role the DOD plays in identifying networks and informing those decisions, the threshold for an organization to receive our attention with respect to terrorist financing action, and given the current environment, should that strategy and threshold being revisited? Would you say that counter-threat financing efforts are a primary, secondary or tertiary concern of our military and intel community? Finally, how effective have our economic pressures been to date and what is your assessment of the ISIL Counter-Financing Working Group?

Dr. KAGAN. I am not familiar with the specific threat-finance activities in which the U.S. Government is currently engaged, and so have no ability to respond directly to most of these questions. It is important to keep in mind, however, that threat-finance activities are extremely unlikely to have a major impact on ISIS as long as the group retains control of a large and populated area with its own natural resources. Threat finance activities have rarely been decisive against any significant opponent, but they are particularly ill-suited to one that can tax people and smuggle oil, as well as ancient artifacts—to say nothing of the ISIS traffic in human beings.

It is nevertheless valuable to do everything we can to disrupt the global financial networks that support ISIS, al Qaeda, and other affiliated movements, and there is generally very little reason not to do so apart from the scarcity of resources the U.S. government can allocate to this problem. It is particularly valuable, I believe, to see threat finance activities within the framework of nexus targeting—seeking targets that cross over from terrorism to human trafficking, narco-trafficking, or other illegal activities. It is often easier to persuade regional partners or the international community to act against human traffickers or drug kingpins than against people we accuse of financing terrorism, and the overlap among these activities is often broad.

Mr. LANGEVIN. What should be the United States' role in fighting Islamic extremism, and what should be the roles of regional actors? Does the U.S. government possess the right tools to fight an ideological war, including information operations authorities? What more should our allies be doing to counter Islamic extremism?

Dr. KAGAN. The U.S. and its regional allies have common interests in defeating Islamist extremism that threatens the legitimacy of all states and has brought violence to all communities. The U.S. should play the role of a reliable ally in this fight. We should provide resources necessary to help our partners, including ground forces when and where they are required and can operate effectively. We should also provide the full panoply of our intelligence-gathering and analysis to our own warfighters and, with the minimum necessary caveats and restrictions, to our partners. The U.S. does not, in my view, possess the right tools to fight an ideological war on the ideological plane. To begin with, what agency would be responsible for fighting such a war? How, moreover, can the U.S. fight an ideological war while denying that the enemy has a religious-based (if, in my view, heretical) ideology? I do not know whether or not the U.S. government has the right legal authorities to fight such a war because we have not come anywhere close to developing a strategy for such an effort, to my knowledge, worth testing.

Mr. LANGEVIN. How should the United States define and approach the threat of Islamic extremism?

Dr. KAGAN. The U.S. must recognize that violent Islamism is a direct threat to Americans and to our way of life. We should define the threat to include those groups and individuals that seek through violent means to impose their vision of Islam upon unwilling populations when those groups also identify the U.S. or its allies as an enemy that must be attacked. We should be careful not to define this particular threat too broadly. Political Islamism—the idea that extreme versions of Islam can and should be imposed on populations through participation in political processes rather than through violence—is also a threat to us, our allies, and Muslims. But responding to political Islamism requires a very different strategy from the one required to combat violent Islamism. It is a mistake, in my view, to make no distinction between the Muslim Brotherhood and al Qaeda or ISIS. All three are threats, and the purely political groups can and often do create conditions propitious for the development of violent groups within their midst. But we should identify political Islamist parties not as ''enemies'' to be ''defeated'' in a war, but rather as political opponents against whom the U.S. and its partners must operate through the effective use of soft power. The best strategy seeks to drive a wedge between political and violent Islamist groups rather than driving them together by targeting both the same.

Mr. LANGEVIN. What are the risks and/or trade-offs in how U.S. policy and strategy defines and addressed the nature of the Islamic extremism threat?

Dr. KAGAN. I believe I have answered this in the preceding responses.

Mr. LANGEVIN. Our comprehensive strategy to combat ISIL includes undercutting their flow of resources. Shutting down access to revenue, and closing the means by which funds flow to and from ISIL is a critical component of that strategy. The Department of Defense, the Department of State, the Department of the Treasury, the Department of Justice, and other intelligence and national security agencies all play a role in identifying and restricting ISIL's access to revenue, and revenue flows. I am interested to hear your thoughts on the effectiveness of the actions we are taking with respect to counter-threat financing, the role the DOD plays in identifying networks and informing those decisions, the threshold for an organization to receive our attention with respect to terrorist financing action, and given the current environment, should that strategy and threshold being revisited? Would you say that counter-threat financing efforts are a primary, secondary or tertiary concern of our military and intel community? Finally, how effective have our economic pressures been to date and what is your assessment of the ISIL Counter-Financing Working Group?

Mr. FISHMAN. Finances are critical for an organization pursue and achieve its goals. As we know from our policy process, appropriating money is the final indicator that an organization values a particular line of effort. Jihadi groups are no different and we have seen various groups put their money where mouth is in different ways over the years. ISIL is different, however, than jihadi groups like al-Qaeda. Because the group controls so much territory, and such a large population, it is able to fundraise via ''taxation'', the appropriation of businesses, and seizing resources from its enemies. Unlike al-Qaeda, which depended largely on donations from wealthy supporters abroad, ISIL generates most of its money locally. ISIL does obviously have some connections to external entities for raising money. For example, it trades oil and antiquities with smugglers and operatives in both government-controlled Syria, Iraq, and Turkey. While we must crackdown on these networks, it is important to recognize that they represent political alliances as well as economic ones. One reason the Awakening in Iraq was so successful is that we were able to co-opt smugglers that were upset about the Islamic State of Iraq (al-Qaeda in Iraq) stealing their smuggling routes. Unfortunately, I do not think that we will be able to effectively constrain ISIL's fundraising without a significant troops presence on the ground. The incentives of ISIL's economic partners run against collaboration with the United States so long as we are unable to coerce them—and most of those networks operate in the black market. Importantly, jihadis have actively tried to build economic networks that are resistant to external pressure. After the failure of the 1980s Muslim Brotherhood uprising against Hafez al-Assad—Bashar's father—Abu Mus'ab al-Suri wrote a widely-read lessons-learned treatise. One of the key elements was that jihadis must be able to fundraise locally and not be dependent on either foreign governments or foreign supporters, both of whom he considered unreliable partners.

Mr. LANGEVIN. What should be the United States' role in fighting Islamic extremism, and what should be the roles of regional actors? Does the U.S. government possess the right tools to fight an ideological war, including information operations authorities? What more should our allies be doing to counter Islamic extremism?

Mr. FISHMAN. The United States does not have the right tools to fight an ideological war, especially one that is framed as undermining jihadi ideology. We ought to be focused on building an image of the United States and democracy that is positive, open, and appealing to people across the world, regardless of their religious or ethnic background. This is not a matter of acumen with social media, as it is often portrayed in the United States. If you review the Islamic State of Iraq's earliest discussion of social media—Youtube, Facebook, etc—in 2008 and 2009 they largely talk about how they need to learn from the effective social media campaigns of American politicians. It's not about how slick they are with social media. The real issue is that they have a clear message—of violence, domination, and what they consider a utopian vision of a better world. Our problem is that we do not have a clear message; it's hesitant and bound by our larger lack of policy clarity toward the challenges in Iraq and Syria. Of course, our allies must do more on the ideological side as well. Saudi Arabia, which is obviously key to U.S. interests for a range of reasons, is a deep cause of the instability in the Mideast. The promotion of Wahhabi mosques globally as undermined progenitors of more pluralistic visions of Islam and fosters an environment that is easier for ISIL and others of its ilk to exploit. Ultimately, we will not be able to solve this problem without Saudi Arabia facing some of its own demons.

Mr. LANGEVIN. How should the United States define and approach the threat of Islamic extremism?

Mr. FISHMAN. It is important to understand that, historically, not all jihadis have been salafis, but that most jihadis today are salafis. In other words, a particular brand of religious ideology is not a good way to define our enemies. That said, there is simply no denying that the backward-looking version of Islam propagated by many in Saudi Arabia (and elsewhere) implies certain political realities, including sectarianism and antipathy to non-Muslims. The United States should be waging war specifically against militant organizations that threaten U.S. interests directly, but we should also be working with our allies to stop their implicit soft power campaigns against us. The Saudi government tolerates and capitalizes on religious extremism. Even as they help us fight militant groups, they support the ideologues that foster those groups. This is unsustainable and self-defeating.

Mr. LANGEVIN. What are the risks and/or trade-offs in how U.S. policy and strategy defines and addressed the nature of the Islamic extremism threat?

Mr. FISHMAN. There are almost too many tradeoffs to list. Even though religious ideology is central to how most jihadi groups define themselves, the United States should not actively frame our counterterrorism campaign in religious terms. We have to be able to walk and chew gum at the same time. We must recognize the ideological foundation of these movements, but our communication efforts are not particularly nuanced. Walk softly (and do not mention Islam very often) but carry a big stick (by empowering moderates who criticize jihadis and cracking down on primarily Saudi efforts to promote destructive ideology). It is important to remember that jihadis kill far more Muslims than they do Americans. With that in mind, we might want to look at terms like ''takfiris'' (a term that reflects their hatred toward Muslims) or ''kharijites'' (a historical term for a despised Muslim sect that attacked other Muslims). Throughout Muslim history, the religion has been practiced and lived dynamically, by real people. In many periods, the Muslim mainstream was more tolerant of minorities than in European societies. That tradition is being destroyed today, both by the jihadis and by states that fund narrow understandings of one of the world's great religious traditions. One danger of defining our enemies solely in ideological terms, rather than in how they operationalize those ideas politically, is that it may prevent us from working with certain allies. There ARE salafi groups that oppose al-Qaeda; we worked with a number of them in Iraq during the vaunted ''Awakening''. At the end of the day; we are interested in ideas because of what they inspire people to do; it's the actions that count. With that in mind, lets not define our enemies so broadly that we prevent areas of potential collaboration.